Selling The American Dream

*How to enjoy making your living
as a Sales Professional*

Tim Dannelly

Bloomington, IN  Milton Keynes, UK

authorHOUSE®

AuthorHouse™
1663 Liberty Drive, Suite 200
Bloomington, IN 47403
www.authorhouse.com
Phone: 1-800-839-8640

AuthorHouse™ UK Ltd.
500 Avebury Boulevard
Central Milton Keynes, MK9 2BE
www.authorhouse.co.uk
Phone: 08001974150

First published by AuthorHouse 8/24/2006

ISBN: 1-4259-5751-X (e)
ISBN: 1-4259-5750-1 (sc)
ISBN: 1-4259-5749-8 (dj)

Library of Congress Control Number: 2006907481

Printed in the United States of America
Bloomington, Indiana

This book is printed on acid-free paper.

Preface

People continue to pour into America. The opportunity here is beyond that of any other place in the world. You can make more money and have a better life as a laborer in America than the middle class in most other countries.

Americans work hard at their careers. A lot of pride goes into the many professions that make up our great land. Many great Americans work their way from an entry level to the top seat in the boardroom. Some professions require decades of education. Some require multiple certifications. All are important to our free enterprise system.

Of all the professions Americans pursue, the profession of sales is most important. Every walk of life requires a sales professional somewhere in the mix. Someone has to be the person who approaches clients and asks them to buy the goods or services.

Most people don't like the idea of approaching people and asking them for money. When your child is involved in a fundraiser, you often end up buying enough products to make the teacher happy rather than exposing your child to all those people who might say no. As a culture, we don't like being rejected or refused. We prefer having things our way. So very few of us enter the world of selling.

If you're reading this book you obviously are drawn to a sales career. Congratulations! You're different from your friends and neighbors. Fewer than 20% of Americans are comfortable in the sales profession. But those who enter sales and enjoy it end up doing very well for themselves.

Most people in sales don't make huge amounts of money. But all people in sales have more freedom and more security in their future than any other profession. That's a bold statement and a true one. Selling is selling and once you master the art, you can sell any product or service in any town of this great country.

The purpose of this book is to help you determine if selling is your calling, and if it is, to give you the tools you'll need in order to succeed in a sales career. I admit you won't find much negative information regarding the sales business in this book – just ask your friends and they can fill you in on how bad it is to be a salesman – but you will find a candid report on the life of a sales professional.

The tools necessary for a person to succeed in sales are present in the bulk of this book. Most salespeople in America only receive training from their company, and that training is usually product knowledge training. While you need to know everything about your product, you also need to know how to sell.

Conducting Sales Seminars all over our great country, I encounter people who have been sales professionals for years and who have no idea why they are succeeding or, worse yet, who are failing and don't know why. The corrective action when a sales person begins to experience a low closing ratio is usually for management to put more pressure on the salesperson. That's about as smart as discovering you're lost and speeding up. If what you're doing isn't working, doing it under pressure is just going to make it worse.

This book is designed to show you how to sell. That begins with traits of successful salespeople and continues with an exact procedure for any sales call. Then you'll read how to determine which clients you should call on and what to do when clients are confrontational.

Special chapters are dedicated to my friends in the automotive and real estate sales arena. All selling is important, but these two industries touch every family in America and their success greatly affects our economy and the quality of our personal lives.

Selling is the last frontier for a person who wants to make something of their life with little or no initial investment. You don't have to come from a wealthy family to succeed in a sales career. Many sales professionals you meet will have plenty of formal education. Some will not. Both groups have the same opportunity at a successful and rewarding life in a sales career. Because, in selling, it's up to you to succeed.

Thanks for buying my book! If you've attended one of my Sales Seminars, thanks for that too! Mostly though, thanks for entering the world of selling. America is a better place every time someone decides to do what the original Americans did back in the 1700's – to take a stand in the marketplace and to help others get your products.

God bless America and God bless you!

Contents

CHAPTER ONE

Why Choose Sales as a Career

Charlie The American Success Story

About thirty years ago, Charlie was a young heavy equipment salesman in North Carolina. He drove hundreds of miles some days working diligently, establishing his account list and making sure his clients got all the heavy equipment they needed. His company expected him to reach certain goals and he was faithful to do so. Sales were good during some months, and during others they were great.

The office Charlie worked from was tasked with selling a modest volume of business. The manager was careful to make sure Charlie and his peers always closed sufficient sales so the office quota was met. With training, direction and incentives, the manager routinely pressed the sales team toward the goal.

Charlie called on a customer one day and discovered a massive undertaking was about to happen. This project would require more heavy equipment than anyone from his office had ever sold. Charlie made the visit to the client and after much careful investigation; he and the client put the order together on paper. When Charlie approached his boss with the order, the boss was unable to fill the order since the office did not have access to that volume of equipment. The boss sent him on up the line to company headquarters.

The order was filled at headquarters and Charlie became an icon in that industry. That event had a very positive financial and emotional impact on him personally. He soon found himself in his own business. Another successful fellow soon joined Charlie in some of his undertakings and it seemed everything Charlie touched turned to gold.

At a time when the tire business was highly competitive he opened a store selling tires and performing automotive maintenance and repairs. His salesmanship and good business practices soon enabled him to open another store in a nearby town and to secure a major tire franchise.

Charlie became a legend in that franchise as he added store after store. Through good economic times and bad, Charlie's tire stores succeeded and grew.

Today, Charlie has sold his company of over 40 stores to his employees. I run into Charlie from time to time and sometimes we'll visit for a minute. I'm always in awe of this epitome of the American Dream. Though he's a humble man, he's a self-made millionaire. He has provided a nice life for his family and he's still not at retirement age. His many employees, across two states, also enjoy the fruits of his labor. Charlie has done more than feed his family, he has helped countless other sales professionals achieve the American Dream.

And it all started because Charlie was a salesman calling on accounts and making sure clients got everything they needed.

How Many Salesmen Can There Be?

Like pioneers on the frontier of 18th and 19th century America, salespeople are on a frontier with unlimited potential. Stories of ordinary people who left humble beginnings and entered a sales career resulting in great wealth are told in every town. In almost every organization, it is the sales professionals who earn the great income. The profession of sales is one of only a few careers available to people regardless of education level, race, gender or background.

Why then doesn't everybody get into a career in sales? The answer is pretty simple and very true. A sales career is not for everybody.

The goal of this book is to empower sales people with techniques and encouragement so that they will excel at their craft. You'll read several times, selling is a mental business. And you'll come to realize that attitude is key to succeeding in a sales career. If you are comfortable with the lifestyle of a sales career, the words in this book will help you achieve more and enjoy it. If you aren't comfortable with the lifestyle of a sales career, nothing can help you reach your full potential in that arena.

Go For It!

Most sales professionals are self-starters. Many of them work from home or out of their vehicles. If you like independence, you'll love selling for a living. The more you sell, the less you hear from your sales manager.

If you find yourself constantly trying to avoid the office politics where you work or if you find you are doing all the work while others visit or loaf, you'll love being a commissioned sales person. Sales professionals are busy filling the needs of clients. They don't have time to sit around in the office. If you know a sales person who sits around and lollygags, you need to know they already have enough money. Wasting time as sales professionals is the same as throwing money out the window.

Great sales professionals are a lot like Charlie. They have exceeded the expectations of the manager and even the company. They constantly go above and beyond established goals. And their work ethic reflects this mindset.

Often, sales professionals are working far beyond traditional quitting time. On the other hand, they play while others work. That's because successful sales professionals are accomplishment-oriented rather than activity-oriented. Traditional American workers believe you should show up on time, do the same things every day and leave on time. This is an honorable ethic and has made our country great. But sales professionals realize all the discipline in the world is useless until the customer signs a contract and issues a check.

Sometimes it takes a week of long hours for a salesperson to get one check from a client. Sometimes it takes 10 minutes. It always takes the right question, asked at the right moment. If you pride yourself in all the hours you work, sales may not be for you. On the other hand, if you find great satisfaction in achieving things, you think like successful sales professionals.

Show Me The Money

Money is a good reason to enter a sales career. There is absolutely no income cap in the sales arena. Don't get me wrong, many managers and even some companies are jealous of the high income that can suddenly come to sales professionals. So they will try to limit the income potential. This is amazingly unwise, since the principal of selling is that the more you sell the more you earn. In most companies, the top earner is one of the sales professionals. As long as sales people are earning high commissions, the company is able to function because large amounts of money are flowing in.

A wealthy fellow owned a small market radio station. The radio station owner was feeling the pinch of a weak economy. Each month, the owner had to supplement the station revenue in order to make expenses. Since he was not a radio person by trade and since he lived in another town, he didn't understand exactly what was causing the problem but knew it was only getting worse. The owner desperately needed to stop this process and was willing to do anything to get the station back on track as a profitable business. He hired a new manager to do whatever it took to turn things around. They agreed the manager would be paid a salary, plus a handsome percentage of the profits. Frankly, the owner didn't care what he had to do or how much the manager was to make. He simply wanted the problem to go away.

The manager worked night and day getting the station equipment operating correctly, making the signal strong and clear. He hired, fired, trained and honed the staff until every person was performing at peak. From that point, the manager focused his efforts on the sales staff, maximizing their production and effectiveness. Within a few months, the station started making a very notable profit. After a year of increasing sales revenues and decreasing problems, the owner took a look at the figure on the manager's monthly check. The owner talked with some other radio station owners who paid their managers far less than he was paying this fellow and decided to approach the manager with a new compensation package.

Reasoning that other managers made far less than he was being paid, the owner told the manager he was going to lower his compensation. The manager reacted like you would, or any person would, and didn't agree. The owner exercised his American right and dismissed the manager, replacing him with someone who would work for far less money. Within a year, the sales staff had been hired by other businesses and the station was right back where it had been when the turn-around manager was hired.

This happens in the sales business. Leadership individuals who do not understand the principals of selling and the capability of disciplined salespeople will make big promises, thinking they'll never have to pay the piper. And when the bill comes due, they will send the gift horse packing. People who get results are envied. And when they make more money than the boss, they're often dismissed.

What an interesting problem – making too much money! How often do you notice that you're doing all the work and making the same amount of money, or even less than your peers in the office? If you're on commission, the more you sell the more you make.

Here's the most amazing money fact about selling for a living; salespeople are not financially motivated.

We all want more money than we already have. We even want our children to have a better life than we do. But successful salespeople are not motivated by money. They are motivated by the desire to win.

That's why salespeople will work extra hard at closing sales when they are in the running for the top sales award. That's why they press for a bonus. That's why they try to sell more this year than last year. The competitive nature of sales professionals causes them to consistently excel.

Some Prefer The Security Of A Salary

Everybody needs salespeople. That's the beauty of this profession. Nothing happens until somebody sells something. Until a product is sold, everything is a liability. Materials cost, labor costs and shipping costs. There is no positive cash flow until somebody buys the product. And nobody buys anything until somebody asks him or her to.

Small business owners often learn this painful lesson. You can make the very best gadget ever made by human hands but if you don't know how to sell it, business grinds to a halt.

Once a sale takes place, all the employees can be paid and all the materials can be purchased to make more products. Frankly, the entire company is at the mercy of the sales staff. If your company is staffed with an outstanding force of sales professionals, your job is secure in that company. But if your sales office is filled with misguided or unproductive salespeople, or if there are too few salespeople to generate the necessary revenue, your company is headed for trouble.

There is really no security in a salaried position. Even if you're the very best salaried employee on the staff, and even if you have worked there longer than anyone else, you have no security if sales begin to slide. Just ask anybody who used to work at a factory that closed. Just ask anybody who worked for a mismanaged company that failed.

The real security is in selling. And selling is selling. Successful sales professionals can sell anything.

Are you aware the minimum wage for waiters and waitresses is actually lower than the minimum wage for other employees? That's because they earn tips, based upon how well they serve their customers. In other words, those who wait tables are sales professionals! If you've ever waited tables, you have a keen understanding of the principals of commissioned sales. The better you are at meeting and exceeding client's expectations, the more money you will make. The more clients you can serve, the more money you will make. Easy to understand, isn't it! Yet the cook is content to work for 50 dollars an hour while the wait staff can be making over $500.00 an hour!

Many great sales people started as wait staff. There they learned the security of controlling one's destiny. In a sales career, you will be responsible for serving enough clients to earn the income you desire. And the more you sell, the more income you will earn.

You'll find that some of your best clients will offer you an opportunity on their sales staff. You'll find offers coming your way all the time, once you are known as a professional salesperson that gets the job done for your company.

Sales professionals sometimes move from job to job because there are so very many opportunities for real sales professionals. Even in the rare circumstance when a sales professional is fired, they are soon hired by another sales organization.

Sales people are not limited to a given field, such as car sales or real estate sales. If you can sell advertising, you can sell cars. If you can sell cellular plans, you can sell airplanes. If you can sell hamburgers, you can sell real estate.

I've sold enlistments in the Air Force, life insurance, education at an institution of higher learning, radio and television advertising, new automobiles, real estate, computer software and hardware, the full line of products in a very special retail store in Burkburnett Texas, and professional sales and leadership training. Since 1968, I've never missed a day of working due to the absence of a sales opportunity.

Beyond The Sales Force

Selling is a career with unlimited growth potential. As you've read, the income potential is unlimited. But some of us like other perks more than we like a fat paycheck. Some wish to move up in an organization and become managers or superintendents. Still others wish to own their own business.

Most successful managers have a sales background or, at the very least, practice the principals of selling people on following. Since selling is selling, the art of convincing a client to purchase is the same as the art of convincing an employee to work. The manager reads the employee and determines what it will take to earn their commitment to company goals and standards. Then they communicate that information to the employee and ask the employee for that commitment.

Many business owners got their 'stake' as a result of sales commissions. Some actually sold the bank on investing in their business.

Why choose sales as a career? Because it is the most secure career!

CHAPTER TWO

Qualities of a Professional Salesperson

Frank The Salesman

In 1968, I met Frank. He was the manager of a Western Auto store in Burkburnette, Texas. As a young Air Force Sergeant with a wife and a rented home, I needed a part time job. Frank hired me and taught me what I needed to know in order to meet the needs and expectations of the clientele.

In 1968, the Western Auto store in Burnburnette was like a super General Store. All the expected items were there – tires, batteries, air conditioners, televisions and even home appliances. But that old store also sold furniture and bedding. We had it all. The big super stores were not yet around, except for a place over in Wichita Falls called White Front. We were downtown next door to the grocery store and across the street from the café.

On a given Saturday, the store would resemble a shopping mall. By the way, no shopping malls were within 100 miles of Burkburnette! People packed the place from 8 in the morning to 8 in the evening. And they bought! I've seen the cash register literally packed with bills on a good Saturday.

Frank taught me how to listen to customers. He reasoned that if you'd just listen to the customer, you'd make the sale lots faster. He had a way of asking customers a question or two, and then suddenly the customer would start talking like they were at a family reunion.

He taught me to sell what the customer wanted and needed, not what I wanted them to have. He believed customers came to the store to buy something, rather than to simply hang out or browse. Frank was right. When he talked with a customer they always ended up buying something.

Color television was becoming affordable and the Dallas Cowboys used to play on some Saturdays in those days. On game days, we sold lots of TV's! We always had comfortable chairs in front of the TV's and in those days, if a man used your TV to watch the game he felt he should buy it.

Frank had an eternal smile. He looked like a movie star anyway, but he could smile and calm the most savage customer. Whenever a customer asked him for help, he dropped everything and took care of them. He was a genuinely nice man that everybody in Burkburnette liked. And they all bought from the Western Auto store.

In 1971, I was transferred to Richmond Virginia to sell for the Air Force as an Air Force Recruiter. Although Recruiting was the opportunity of a lifetime to me, I hated to say good-bye to Frank. He was like a dad and a professor all rolled into one. I knew he had taught me a lot about selling, but I had no idea where it would lead.

In my life, I've had some great sales training. Air Force Recruiting School in San Antonio gave me a procedure for selling that has proven consistently successful. Along the way, a few corporations have taught me techniques that have helped close many sales. Friends in the Sales Training business have helped me constantly learn new ways to apply old truths.

But Frank was the man who opened the door of opportunity to my life as a salesman and encouraged me until I became confident. I never forgot his practical approach to helping customers become owners and his encouraging way of managing his sales force. As a sales manager myself, I often found myself wondering how Frank would handle a given situation.

In 1984, I was living in San Antonio and had a speaking engagement for a school district in Wichita Falls so I drove over to Burkburnette and visited Frank. The Western Auto store was gone, thanks to the new big super stores, and Frank was running a building supplies store. When I walked in the door, there was that big movie star smile and that magnetic way he had of starting a conversation. After a few minutes of telling him the news of my family, I took a deep breath and thanked him for introducing me to the world of sales and for preparing me to excel. In the best way I could muster, I told him his patience and skill had enabled me to provide for my family beyond my wildest dreams.

You should have seen his face. He thanked me but immediately started asking about the products and services I had been selling. From my training and sales experience, I soon realized what he was doing. He didn't want a big fuss made about him. His reward came in doing what he did – helping customers solve their problems and achieve their goals. What a humble man! What a customer-centered man! What a salesman!

Some have asked me if I believe some people are naturally born salesmen. I have to say I don't. Selling is a learned art rather than a natural talent. But I do believe some learn the process and adapt to the lifestyle of a sales career more easily than others.

Pull For The Customer

Sales professionals believe the client will really be better off once they own their product or service. They believe their product is the very best available. Often you'll meet a sales professional who is intentionally inconvenienced, by working far from home or even for less money, so they can sell a particular product.

Sales professionals are compassionate. With a sincere genuine interest in the customer, they pull for the customer to win. When the customer wins, everybody wins! When the company wins at the customer's expense, the end is near. Because the company needs the customer's money in order to keep the doors open and pay the bills.

Sometimes, pulling for the customer to win requires extreme bravery on the part of the sales professional. The customer may refuse your proposal because they don't realize how much they'll benefit when they say "yes". In other words, they need to 'know' more in order to make the purchase. If you are truly going to believe that when a customer says, "No" it means, "know", you're going to need thick skin and lots of patience.

Keep Your Mind On Business

Sales professionals need to stay focused. The rejection rate in some types of sales is extremely high. If you lose focus of how many contacts are necessary in order to secure sufficient closed sales, you will begin to think about all the people saying "no", rather than how close you are to achieving your goal. Since selling is a mental business, successful sales professionals are disciplined and keep their minds on business.

Sales professionals work hard at being congenial and charismatic. They dress for success. So a sales person who lacks self-discipline will easily become distracted by the natural reactions of clients to the smooth moves of a suave communicator. Most extremely successful sales professionals keep their personal life at home and their business life at work. Mixing the two almost always results in one, or both, being damaged.

Along with being mentally focused, sales professionals must be good managers of their time. You are paid for your time. Clients will often even say to you, "Thank you for your time." With proper prioritizing, maximum earnings are possible when selling any product. The reverse is also true. Time is money. Wasting time in the sales business means wasting money.

When paperwork is necessary as a part of the sales process, sales professionals accomplish it carefully and accurately. They apply the principal of touching each piece of paper only once. Not only does it take more time to fill out the same paperwork twice, clients who were happy the first time they signed all the forms suddenly become very demanding when called in to re-accomplish the same paperwork.

A Good Money Manager

Salespeople are not financially motivated! If they were, salespeople would all be rich. Most are not. Above all, salespeople wish to win! Salespeople will forgo a well-deserved full commission in order to win a sale.

When you bought your last car or truck, chances are the salesman did not sell it to you for the full asking price. You ended up negotiating a lower price. While your salesman was negotiating with you, he was also talking the company into taking less for the vehicle. When you thought he as in the back room telling jokes with his buddies, he was actually convincing the manager to make less profit on the vehicle you were buying. Sales revenues determine the manager's commission check and also govern whether he keeps his job so he isn't thrilled when a salesman says the profit on a transaction is going to be less than expected. Many times, the salesperson will end up in the hot seat because he is lowering the price of a product. Yet he does so because every customer who ever took a breath of air feels every price of every product is too high! So the salesman gives in to the customer and works on the boss until an agreement is reached. Why would a person expend all that effort and endure all that stress when the result will be a lower commission check? Because he wants to WIN! The salesman loses if the customer doesn't buy, but if the customer buys, he WINS!

Salespeople are forever talking management into running a special package or reduced price sale in order to cause more customers to purchase. Since this is the case, salespeople often find themselves more than a dollar short on payday. Because salespeople are positive by nature, they view a short payday as a one-time occurrence and can easily get themselves behind the financial eight ball.

Wise sales people follow a strict budget. If you follow an annual budget, fat months may thrill you or short months may upset you but the "feast and famine" illness will not strike you. Retail salespeople do very well during the weeks leading up to Christmas but may not fare so well during the cold winter months when shoppers stay home by the fire. Automotive salespeople do well in late summer as the new models start to arrive and discounts are applied to last year's model but they dread January when customers are facing their credit card statements from Christmas.

Now you're beginning to see why salespeople must live on a budget! When you excel and get the whopper bonus, bank it! When the company is giving away the products and your bonus check looks like your babysitter's income statement, head for the savings account and stay current with your financial obligations. Trust me, this day will come.

Make A Declaration of Independence

The independent nature of sales professionals sets them apart! Many sales professionals in the United States work from their automobiles or from an office in their home. In the late 1970's several of my associates in corporate recruiting were working from home. Some of us work from our laptops and cell phones in all sorts of places. A professional salesperson does not require a fully staffed and furnished office. All they need is a point of contact.

Whether you're an inside or outside sales professional, you must be an independent thinker who functions well on your own. If you're so goal-oriented that you'll go to where the client is, whenever the client can meet with you and help the client accomplish what has never been accomplished, you possess the qualities of a professional salesperson!

It serves to reason that if you're working while others play, you also will be playing while others work. Often, others at your house will be heading to school or work at a time of day when you don't have appointments. If you love to golf or shop, or if you are a disciplined runner, you will often find yourself doing these things during traditional 'working hours'. Independent sales professionals who are accomplishment-oriented feel no guilt when they take an hour in the middle of the day to go shopping.

As long as you are exceeding the expectations your company and your manager have for you, you can do whatever pleases you with your time. Of course, until you reach the sales numbers set by your superiors, they expect you to work from the time you wake up until you go to sleep.

Expectations are usually based upon the history of your company or industry. If you are a driven person, exceeding expectations is not an overwhelming task. Most people are driven to make a living, not to make a killing so expectations are usually right down the middle. On the rare occasion that a salesperson feels the bar is set too high, they are usually able to work it out with their manager. Selling is selling, even when you're selling your sales manager.

Honor

The Honor Code of some military organizations reads in part, *I will not lie, cheat or steal, nor will I tolerate those who do.* Perhaps your mom told you, "If you lie down with dogs, you'd get up with fleas." Or, "People judge you by the company you keep."

When I entered the car business, lots of my well-meaning friends said things like this to me. On several pages of this book, you'll read about people in the car business for which I had a high regard. But isn't that business known for shady dealings? It only takes one or two people, given enough attention, to give an entire industry a bad name.

People say car salesmen are crooks, but most car salesmen are actually hard working ordinary people who are trying the best they can to serve their customers with honor. By the same token, you'll hear people say they trust their preacher fully, but some preachers are actually far from being trustworthy.

The honor is not in the profession. The honor is in the professional.

Customers naturally doubt the truthfulness of salespeople. They see the salesperson as being paid to sell the product and willing to do or say whatever it takes. This does not mean customers are bad people or that salespeople are out to get you. It simply means sales professionals must earn the trust of clients.

That's why repeat customers spend more money and allow you to make a higher profit. The hurdle of trust is no longer in the sales process. The client can focus on how the product or service will benefit them rather than wonder if the sales person is treating them fairly. Your honor is key in building a relationship with clients and molding them into the faithful customers who will feed your family year after year.

Faithful customers will not question your integrity. They'll trust you to always be truthful with them and fair in your dealings. Your honor must be a part of your personal character and must only deepen. It only takes one breech of this trust to destroy a relationship and lose the account.

What You See Is What You Get

Many in our culture are people of expression. They are who they are. If you don't like the way they dress or if you don't like their opinions or their music, that's your own tough luck. "Deal with it", they say! While the American culture is becoming a culture of hermits, with our hands-free cell phones and PDA's, we're less and less concerned with how our actions affect the lives of others. Sales professionals can never go to this place.

Sales professionals must be magnetic, winsome people. They are constantly seeking prospects for their products or services, which means they are constantly meeting new and different people. People who tend to have flamboyant lifestyles or who feel the need to be egocentric or confrontational have a hard time in the sales profession. Making a fashion statement, for instance, is fine if you're attending some event or going to a party, but it only draws unwanted attention in a sales environment. It's difficult to get your client to focus on your product if your clothing or personal grooming is overwhelming.

Sales professionals just naturally put their best foot forward all the time. No wonder they end up in management! The manager is generally the 'professional-looking' one of the staff. As a professional sales trainer, one reason I love presenting Sales Seminars is that everybody attending is so well dressed and their conduct is so winsome!

Society has some nicknames for people who put their best foot forward while the rest of the world is busy having 'casual Friday' every day of the week. You may hear sales professionals referred to as peacocks or show-offs. Of course, you must realize this is nothing more than a jealous reaction to your professional appearance. Nothing sets the tone like your appearance. The slob who dresses down often wishes they had the taste or the bravado to dress like a professional every day. Rather than compliment you on your appearance and the confidence you possess, they poke fun or ostracize you.

The more you sell and the higher you rise, the more jealousy will rear its ugly head. Everybody wants your money and notoriety, but nobody wants to do the work required to earn it. So it's easier to just be jealous. Sales people will be jealous of you when you exceed their achievements. Other people within the company will be jealous of your freedom as a professional. Sometimes this will be pleasant, with some friendly joking. Sometimes it will be brutal, with people wishing to expose some flaw in your character so management will send you packing.

When jealousy or conflict comes your way, be kind and get away from it as soon as possible. Since we are the sum total of our thoughts, degrading information about us is nothing more than brain damage.

Sales professionals are in a mental business so we cannot afford to load our mind with negative information about ourselves, especially when it is driven by jealousy. Be nice. Then be gone! Don't make a habit out of defending your character. King Solomon once wrote that you should always let someone else do that anyway.

Jealousy displayed or expressed by others is actually an asset. It keeps you on your toes! Your accounts must always be in order and your conduct above reproach. If you put your best foot forward and live by the Honor Code you'll not only do well as a sales professional, you'll do well in every part of life.

You'll have a clear conscience before God and man.

CHAPTER THREE

Who Needs Salespeople

The Leader Of The Pack

In the dog-eat-dog marketplace that is America, things get heated up. One reason people shy away from a sales career is that they have a negative impression of sales professionals in general. It isn't fair to judge an entire pack by one or two dogs.

Some are Hot Dogs. A Hot Dog in the sales world is here today and gone tomorrow. The Hot Dog often breezes in out of nowhere and zooms to the top of an organization. If you've worked with this energetic pup, you've had your clients stolen and your patience tested. All they can seem to focus on is getting one more sale on the board, regardless of what's required or who benefits. Your discomfort caused by the Hot Dog is usually intense, but also short-lived. Hot Dogs have no staying power. They breeze in, burn up the woods then leave town.

The Top Dog is similar to the Hot Dog but has more commitment. As long as they are #1, they will stay with an organization and never miss a day. Top Dog is always either #1 or #2 on the Sales Board and will do anything to stay in first place. Count on Top to work hard and serve his clients well. But also know that, when threatened by another salesperson who is working hard and enjoying a good streak of business, this mutt will give away products, falsify reports, steal deals and even resort to throwing an old fashioned fit to remain at the top of the Sales Board. The Top Dog will even quit his long time position in an organization if superior sales professionals join the team. He cannot abide simply being a member of the team. He must always be number one, for he is the smartest Dog in the Kennel (in his own mind).

Be on guard for the Attack Dog. With his zealous approach to selling, he hides and lunges for the client's throat with little or no respect for the client as a person. He has very little return business since he runs clients away after one good cleaning of their wallets. He constantly asks for decisions from clients who have been given only a small part of the required information. When clients ask for more information, Attack Dog spins into action with insults and pressure beyond description. He knows hundreds of trick closes and ways to detain the client until "yes" is the only possible response. Attack Dog has many crafty ways to add income to each sale without necessarily adding value. He has a pay-up-or-get-out mentality. Attack Dog has lost sight of the fact that clients meet with him because they already like, and may even want, his product or service – they don't require trickery or brute force in order to make a decision to buy. Once the neighbors learn about Attack Dog, they simply avoid the establishment where he's located until he leaves. This sometimes takes a long time since his manager is usually scared to death of him, or is involved in routinely using deceptive trade practices himself.

Mad Dog is somewhat like Attack Dog, but more of a stealth operator. Mad Dog does a good job of serving his clients and supporting his team. He works hard and even wins a few sales awards along the way. Then one day, something sets him off. He flies hot, demanding to have his way or else. Sometimes, Mad Dog is set off when his client challenges his proposals or even buys somewhere else. Rather than try his best to retain the client as a customer for life, Mad Dog runs in circles and foams at the mouth seeking vengeance on the client in some way. By the way, if you ever sell to Attack Dog or Mad Dog, watch out! They have absolutely no respect for other sales professionals since they believe all people working in sales are like them.

Then there's the Lazy Dog. He waits at the sales manager's door for a bone. He waits for customers to surrender. Old Lazy often says things to his clients like, "When you're ready to buy, call me". He seldom gets face-to-face with a client. The only time Lazy Dog asks for the money with any zest or passion is when he asks his boss for an advance against his commission or when he asks to be put on salary.

The only dog more useless than Lazy Dog is Old Yellow. He never asks for anything. While he actually does make an effort, unlike Lazy Dog, his sales calls and customer contacts consist of lots of beating around the bush with no close. Old Yellow will take a client 10 proposals, complete with slide presentations, samples and a free lunch, without ever asking for a commitment. Lazy Dog and Old Yellow always have a very current resume.

The Preferred Pup

A dog has been the great American pet for generations. I suppose even George Washington had a dog. We like dogs. Americans pay lots of money to purchase, groom and feed their dogs.

When Americans go shopping for products or services, they like familiar territory and faces. People want and need a connection in the sales world. They prefer to buy from an insider. They want to be pampered. They are willing to pay more for the services of a professional. People want dependability, the sort you get from your little dog – the little creature who is always "on" and who never holds a grudge against you.

You never give much thought to what sort of day your dog has had unless you have to take him to the Vet. You don't worry about whether your dog is the most important dog in the neighborhood or whether he's happy in his dog work. He's your pet. You enjoy him, feed him and get on with life.

This is similar to what people want from their connection in the sales world. They don't care, because they cannot understand, about turf wars within the sales staff or whether you're number one this month. They may listen kindly as you complain about your sales manager or boast of your latest achievement, but they're simply being kind. They need you in order to get the product or service you sell. Once they have what they came for, they are thinking about leaving.

A connection in the market is really a lot like Man's Best Friend! The committed professional salesperson meets or exceeds their quota each month, assures a profit for the company, keeps customers for life, and is a team player. Their dealings are always about the customer's wants, needs and expectations. They are loyal to their customers like your dog is loyal to you.

Just as your dog responds to your call, committed sales professionals seem to always know what you need and when you need it. They find ways for you to get the product, even when no one else can get one and even when you think there is no way for you to acquire it! They never hold a grudge because you bought somewhere else or because you argued with them about the price or lost your temper when a service issue arose. Like your faithful dog, they start with a fresh positive outlook each time you do business. How refreshing! And how unusual!

Irresistible Sales Professionals

In the dog-eat-dog world known as the marketplace, one can easily slip into the habit of fighting the other salespeople in order to beat them and win the top spot on the board. Or one can easily slip into the price war that occurs between you and your competitors every day. Your dog has temptations too! He wants to chase around with the other dogs or rip his nemesis to shreds. He may even be doing this as you call for him. If he is, he will soon stop and head for your side. He knows who feeds him.

Wise sales professionals know who feeds them. They know they are not fed by the company, or the sales board, or the other people on their sales team or by the competition – they are fed by their clients. They focus their efforts on the client's needs, desires, likes, dislikes, expectations, and even on ways of solving the client's problems before they become problems.

I don't know about you, but I cannot resist a salesperson like this. I'll buy whatever they're selling! You're probably agreeing with me by now. Since you probably work hard at doing a good job for your clients, you appreciate the excellent personal service provided by another professional. Sales professionals make the best customers. Sales professionals can sense when they are being half-served or when the person across the table is taking shortcuts. We have heard all the excuses not to buy so we appear to have great sales resistance. But when sales professionals encounter another professional, they lower their guard and purchase!

My dentist and his staff are excellent sales professionals. They are always happy to see me. They smile and call me by name. They even call a day or two prior to our appointment to remind me of the impending event! Each procedure we go through is in my best interest. Occasionally, I've had to see my dentist for emergency needs when I've had no appointment or even after business. I never gave much thought to whatever it was they had to do in order to serve me; I simply remember they took care of the situation. It's never about my dentist; it's always about me! They never let me settle for second best when making dental decisions. Then never let me suffer as a result of saving a few dollars. When they ask for the money, they ask boldly with a smile! They know the value of their service far exceeds the small investment. I never give much thought to how much money my dentist makes or how well he pays his staff. Come to think of it, I've never tried to negotiate with my dentist either! How about you? Have you negotiated with your dentist, or your heart surgeon, or your local EMT? The work is worth the fee. Because it benefits me!

Yes, the dog-eat-dog world of selling is challenging. But if you are called to a career in sales, the challenges are outweighed by the benefits. Whatever you are paid, and sales professionals tend to be well paid, your bonus is the gratitude of your clients. Just as a mechanic can't do dental work, people need salespeople in order to get the things they want and need in order to live their lives.

Sales Professionals Move Our Economy

Without sales professionals, our entire economy stops.

Companies need salespeople in order to move their products and maintain cash flow. If you are already working in a sales career, you probably cringe when your company president wants to interact with your best client. If your company president is a seasoned selling professional, of course, you don't worry at all. But most executives are not sales oriented. They're used to calling shots, rather than filling needs and soothing feelings.

Independent small business owners need sales professionals because these entrepreneurs are often so passionate about their product or service that they are unable to handle routine customer concerns. Sales professionals quickly learn that disagreeing with a client is no way to get the order. But when you've spent your life coming up with a concept and turning it into reality, and when you've invested all you have into a business, you don't care to hear some customer tell you they saw a better one down the street.

Buyers need salespeople in order to get the goods and services they are looking for. How many times have you shared the name of a friend in this business or that business? We all want to buy from an insider. Another reason buyers need salespeople is their requirements and the product's availability often do not match. Creativity is a trait salespeople have had since our craft was first practiced. Speaking of creativity, how many times have you helped a client find a creative way to finance your product? Sales professionals are the reason we have the ability to finance automobiles and homes today.

The financial world needs salespeople in order to sell their loans and business accounts. Not only are salespeople in the form of loan officers working directly inside the bank, many loan transactions are occurring at the suggestion of sales professionals. If you are selling boats for $10,000.00 and constantly encountering customers who can't afford to write a check for that amount, it isn't long before you enlist a banker to sell loans to your customers.

The government needs salespeople in order to generate revenue through sales of goods and services so taxes will be paid on that money. No only are you doing your American duty by paying your own taxes on your ever-increasing sales income, you're helping all the people mentioned on this page earn enough money to be obligated pay their own taxes.

The more people on commission, the more money America's economy will produce. And the more money produced, the more jobs created.

Yes, America needs sales professionals.

CHAPTER FOUR

What To Know Before Applying For A Sales Position

Step By Step - Here's How!

If you were to apply for a position as a pilot with a major airline, you would need to show proof of your ability to fly a plane. If you wanted to drive professionally, you'd need a license. Whatever you do in America, you need to know how. You'll never land a job without possessing the necessary skill. For some strange reason, this doesn't apply if you're interested in a sales position.

People are hired to fill sales positions every day with little or no idea of the anatomy of a sale. Even some sales managers have no idea of what steps sales professionals must take in order to help people to decide to purchase. Most sales people have little or no sales training. They rely on their drive and their wits. Even when they succeed, they don't know exactly what they did to close so many sales.

When you have felt pressure put on you by a salesperson, it has been because that sales person did not know how to sell. Selling is not trickery. It is not forcing people to make decisions by lying to them. Selling is not about inflating, then lowering the price. It is not about clowns and balloons and hotdogs and gimmicks. Selling is an organized and intentional approach to helping people achieve a goal or gain an advantage.

Since few sales organizations train their sales staff in the basic techniques of professional selling, few sales professionals function at their potential. And if you understand the principals of selling and follow the steps to successfully selling, you will always sell more than your contemporaries who do not. The rest of the pack will use trickery or resort to buying business by constantly lowering their price.

Parting with money is a hard thing for Americans. They love to dine, play, travel, purchase and enjoy, but they don't like to pay! Consequently, lots of industries use low price as their drawing card. Some actually keep dropping their price during the sales process until the customer finally says yes.

Customers actually seldom buy because of price. They buy because they perceive the product or service will fill their need or satisfy their want. Why else would an entire culture own vehicles that cost more than their parents first home? We want what we want, when we want it. Low price only works on impulse purchase and seldom brings repeat and referral business. No man wants to be known for the cheap engagement ring he gave his wife.

Since money is the vehicle by which we acquire all our nice things, sooner or later any sales conversation comes back to price. The sales professional that satisfies the wants or fills the needs of a client may have to address price, but they will not lose a sale if the benefit is of sufficient value in the client's mind. Customers often discuss price for lack of a better topic. But if the product or service is something with absolutely no value or use to them, the lowest price in the market is meaningless. On the other hand, people gladly pay up for valuable things.

How do you determine what your client is thinking? How do you know his expectations of your product or service? How do you know whether your client can afford your product or if it will do the job for him? What will it take to earn his business?

If you know the answers to these questions, you'll succeed at selling anything. Sufficient product knowledge and professional selling skills have enabled successful sales professionals for centuries.

Successful sales professionals follow a plan when they sell. Much like a surgeon or a pilot, they start at a precise place, follow an exact plan and arrive at a predetermined goal.

How Do You Begin A Sales Call?

Salespeople call on clients every day to pitch their products or services. Quite often, the client will ask something like, "What's on special?" or say, "Give me your best price!" and the salesman will follow the lead with their best foot forward.

If you went over to your best friend's house to borrow something, you wouldn't dive right in to your reason for being there. You'd spend a few minutes visiting or chatting about totally unrelated subjects. This is a very effective technique for beginning a sales call.

Take A Few Minutes To Visit On A Casual Level

Two Professional Speakers sat down for lunch together on a holiday. They had looked forward to this meal together since both had lots of questions for the other, hoping to enhance their businesses. They agreed they needed to meet in a restaurant where a lengthy meeting could be accommodated.

Once they started talking, hardly a second passed in silence. As one completed a thought, the other would jump in with a new thought. Question after question was vigorously and thoroughly answered. Each gained vital and beneficial information. They even took notes! As they went to their cars, they talked all the way to the parking lot. What a conversation! It went on for over two hours!

Is this typical of your opening conversation with clients? Solid productive talking with little or no prompting! That isn't a fair question, is it? Most people don't care to 'carry the conversation' and most clients have some degree of sales resistance causing them to appear introverted in any conversation with a salesman. So we sales professionals end up having to keep things moving by doing all the talking.

People naturally resist change. If your boss made you read this book for instance, you aren't getting all you can get out of it. You already knew enough about selling and he came along and forced you to change from knowing to learning. You didn't want to change. Neither does your client. Change is very uncomfortable.

That's why some clients are so rude. It isn't that they want to be obnoxious or overbearing egomaniacs, it's that they are in a new and different situation. And that situation is threatening their comfort zone.

When your client enters your store or when you enter your client's office, you bring change. Change generates discomfort. You'll see it in your client's eyes. It's normal for the most talkative client to suddenly shut down when encountered by a salesperson. A salesperson is something new. A change!

The first order of business is to help a client get past the change. Clients want to relax and get past the change too, and later on they'll appreciate your kindness in helping them get past their butterflies. You'll be glad you calmed down too, because doing so will help you think clearly and serve your client more effectively.

Have you ever noticed the way you interact with your friends, compared to how you interact with your acquaintances? You talk with your friends! You only give a little information to acquaintances. Sometimes you and your friends will sit and talk for hours about nothing. But mere acquaintances only share answers to questions or small talk.

How To Get Clients To Talk With You Like Friends

Six words are often used in industries requiring information from others. For instance, you'll find professionals in law enforcement, medical, journalism and counseling walks of life employing these words in conversation quite often. The words are 'who, what, when, where, why and how'. Sentences started with these words result in people sharing information. And the more you follow the answers to these questions with still another 'who, what, when, where, why or how', the more your client will open up to you and the more information they will share.

When you ask a question, wait for the answer. People naturally refrain from conversation if they sense you are willing to do all the talking. If you begin a sentence with 'who, what, when, where, why or how' and wait for an answer, the client will tell you the answer. Listen to the answer. Try to mentally outline the main thought the client is conveying to you. As you follow up with even more 'who, what, when, where, why or how' questions, take a sincere genuine interest in the client and what they are sharing.

One very noticeable result of such a method of starting a sales call is that your client will visibly relax. And you will become interested in what the client is saying so you will also relax. When your client is relaxed, he is more candid. He will tell you what you need to know in order to do your job. When you are relaxed, you are able to think clearly and listen better and, best of all, sell more effectively.

Want to see if this really works? The next time you're in a social setting, seek out the most withdrawn individual and ask them how things are going. You know the rest. Just keep following up with sentences that begin with 'who, what, when, where, why or how'. You may have to be very patient at first and there may be some long pauses as you wait for a response but, by and by, they will begin to open up and talk to you. Don't be surprised when they talk your ears off.

After a few minutes of interaction with a relaxed client, you may even find yourself saying, "I've enjoyed talking with you about your grandchildren, but you did say you're looking for some information on a new security system. In order to better serve you, I need to ask a few questions. Would that be alright?"

Professionals Need Information To Serve Clients.

We need certain information in order to serve our clients in the best way possible. The client might miss out on a particular product or service if we never realized they needed it. Before we can sell anything, we must assess the needs and expectations of the client. We must determine that we in fact can solve the client's problems and help the client achieve their goals. So we need for clients to share information.

Unfortunately, many sales interviews are starved for information and the client ends up having to 'think it over', which really means they end up not buying from us. Even when we lower the price several times and recite every bit of information about our product, they still don't buy. Some small concern or question in their mind stops the sales process like a red light stops traffic.

Is This For You Or For Someone Else?

I remember the rainy evening when the lady in the relatively new luxury automobile drove onto the new car lot where I was working. It was about 5 minutes before closing time and we were locking things up. An older salesman watched as she stopped behind a new sport utility vehicle and got out to look at the window sticker. He turned to me and said, "Watch and learn", then strolled out gracefully with his big golf umbrella to cover her. Stepping outside, I could hear the conversation.

"Hi, honey. You like that vehicle?" I could not believe my ears. She certainly looked like a honey, but I could not believe he called her that! But that was nothing! When she told him she would like to test-drive it he replied, "It's closing time and we're just about to turn out the lights. You bring your husband back tomorrow and you can take it out for a spin."

Every person among the decision-makers is important. If a child is sent to your office or store for information on a product, that child is now a part of the decision-makers. Further, they are your only representative to the other decision-makers of that purchase. Successful sales professionals must deal with decision-makers. But you must carefully include all parties as you interact. And it goes without saying that insult to any one of the decision-makers will certainly kill the sale.

Can You Buy Or Are You Wasting My Time?

You are a lot of fun to be around. You're also a very persuasive individual. These two facts naturally follow a sales professional. Once you take a sincere genuine interest in a person, that person will want to spend lots of time talking to you. So few people listen to the words of other people that you will be different as you listen to your client. And you'll be persuading people that your product is the one to own. These are two reasons you must be careful to whom you spend your time selling.

Every person you encounter can buy something. Even if they cannot afford your product, they can afford an inferior product similar to yours. People appreciate the sales professional who helps them get what they are looking for. Do you have a relationship with sales professionals who sell a lesser-priced product similar to yours? This relationship will aid you in always helping every client you serve.

The higher the value of your product or service, the more likely you will encounter clients who want it but cannot buy it. How soon in the sales process do you want to know a client is not capable of buying? And what do you do with a client who cannot buy?

Do you recall those social outings in your young life that turned out badly? I remember going to a dance and asking a very pretty girl to dance. I sort of expected her to turn me down since she was out of my league. She not only told me no, she gave me that look. You know the look! The one that seems to say, "You're the last person on earth I'd dance with!" Who knows whether she was really thinking such a thing? The fact remains, the way she handled the decline left me with negative feelings about her that never went away. I was glad when we moved away and I no longer had to bump into her in the hall at school.

Sometimes you must decline a client for various reasons. A person who cannot buy this year can often buy in the near future. Since you're going to be about building a client list of customers for life, this person is still a prospect.

Suppose the pretty girl had called one of her friends over and said to me, "Thanks for coming over and talking with us! You're very friendly!" Suppose she and her friend had discussed the music and the evening with me. And what if, after a few moments, she had then said to me, "You really should ask my friend to dance! She's a very good dancer!" The pretty girl would have ended up being my friend.

Rather than giving a client a negative report such as, "I'm sorry, you can't buy due to your low credit score", why not say, "Let me introduce you to an associate of mine who specializes in helping my friends do what others think cannot be done." Clients with financial and credit issues are aware of their situation so it seldom comes as a surprise to them when their loan is declined. It does come as a surprise when someone continues to give them the white glove treatment. In the future, their financial picture will likely improve and they will remember that you treated them with respect and helped them make the purchase they want to make.

What's It Going To Take To Earn Your Business?

Almost 40 years ago, I watched a sales training film depicting a scenario of such a situation. The film was over 30 years old at the time but it made a real impression on this young salesman. A fellow wanted to purchase some long underwear but he was particularly concerned that it might itch. Having spent some cold nights in a drafty North Carolina farmhouse as a boy, I could understand this concern. The man went to an upscale department store and asked the sales professional if their long underwear itched. The well-dressed salesman was extremely knowledgeable of the features and benefits of the line of underwear sold in his store, and he was very smooth in his presentation. He even offered the man a substantial discount if he bought several. The shopper seemed almost ready to buy as he paused and intently asked the salesman, "Will these itch?" The salesman related that he didn't honestly know whether they itched since he didn't usually wear that type of underwear, but that this was the finest long underwear on the market. The shopper responded like many customers do when they still have a nagging question in the back of their minds, "I'll think about it. Do you have a card? I'll come back later." And with that, the shopper headed to another store and went through the same process. This cycle repeated itself several times until the man, on his way home, stopped at the local hardware store for some nails. While the clerk was getting the nails, the shopper asked if the store carried long underwear. "We do", the clerk replied, "But it's red and most folks don't want red underwear." The clerk reached up the sleeve of his shirt and pulled out an inch of his own red long underwear to show the unsightly fashion statement. By now you might be ahead of me. The shopper couldn't resist asking the obvious, "Does that red underwear itch?" The clerk replied, "Nope. It doesn't itch at all. But it's red." The customer bought the entire stock of his size. He didn't care if it was red, or what the price was. He simply wanted some underwear that didn't itch. All the talk in the world just went right over his head until someone told him 'it doesn't itch'. Even deeply discounted pricing didn't cause this shopper to buy. He wanted what he wanted and he spent lots of time going from store to store, probably listening to lots of feature and benefit selling. All the while, he was really looking for some underwear that didn't itch. Price was never an issue. He was never the least bit concerned with warranty, product reputation or packing. And the more he heard all the sales talk, the more he really wanted to hear "they won't itch".

You might think it isn't fair for a client to be so fickle. Why didn't he simply say what it would take to do business? I'll tell you why. He didn't know he was supposed to say it. Shoppers are very savvy and focused on what they want. But they are not familiar with the sales process. That's why they need you! Sales professionals provide the service of marrying customers with products and services, based upon the information available. While the salespeople of the world may make factual presentations, they seldom gather information before sharing information. One trait that sets the great American Salesman apart is the way this professional gathers vital information prior to staking any claims.

Some Like It Hot, Some Like It Cold

Many of your clients will be replacing a product similar to yours. They chose that product and paid good money for it. At the moment of purchase, they thought it was the best solution for them. Would you believe some salespeople actually criticize past decisions made by their clients?

The truck salesman who makes negative comments about the trade-in truck his client is driving is making life hard for himself. When he tells the client how much the dealership is willing to pay for the trade-in, the client will actually defend the trade and may even end up driving away in it. If a person cares enough about a product to part with money in order to own it, they will resist being told they made a mistake when they purchased it.

Wise sales professionals begin gathering information about customer preferences by starting where they are – with their current product. "What do you like most about your current lawn mower", the lawn and garden sales professional will ask as the client looks at the lawn tractors on display in his store. And the sales professional will follow up with information seeking 'who, what, when, where, why or how' questions. Each answer the client gives is important since they are truly telling you exactly what they want the new product to do that the old one is already doing.

On the other hand, the customer is shopping because they are ready for a change or because the current product is not getting the job done. "If you could change one thing about your current accounting software, what would it be", asks the software company representative as the comptroller anxiously stops work for a few moments to shop. As the answer comes, the representative again asks the 'who, what, when, where, why or how' questions and waits patiently for each selling point to be laid out by the client.

"How do you plan to use your new vehicle", asks the salesman as the mom reigns in her children. "I'm going to drive it to work on my daily hundred mile commute", she says. I'll bet fuel economy is really important to her! Suppose she had said, "I take the neighborhood kids to school each morning", adding that the school is 8 miles from her house. Maybe seating and safety would become more important. Want to know for sure? Just ask! Knowing how your client plans to use your product or what their expectations are regarding its problem-solving ability is key when we make the sales presentation. We can point out exactly how it will benefit that exact client!

Many sales people dread discussing price. The price of every product and service is far beyond reality. Just ask any of my rural neighbors!

Thirty years ago it was lots cheaper! Why not ask the client how much they plan on investing in the product while you're still gathering information! While the client's response isn't carved in stone, it certainly lets you know what they're thinking regarding the value of your product or service. If your client says they plan to invest $100,000 in their new home and their expectations are for the luxuries of a $175,000 home, you now know you need to educate them in a positive way regarding the difference. On the other hand, if your client thinks a new suit will cost $400 and you can sell them exactly what they like for $200, this will be an easy sale!

As you listen to the client talk about what they like and dislike about their current situation, the proposed use of the new product and the budget they desire to stay within, you begin to realize the client has told you exactly what they expect your product to do for them and exactly what they believe this solution will cost.

Only when you feel you have sufficient information to defend a solution with two or three personal applications to the client, should you proceed to present that solution.

Such A Deal I Have For You!

Ask the client if you are correct in your assumption of the solution to their situation. The Military Recruiter asks, "As I see it, you're looking for training in a solid skill that will provide you a good life-long living. Is that right?" If the Recruiter has listened carefully and is correct in his hypothesis, the client will reply, "That's right!"

Offer your solution in a brief statement that boldly stakes your claim. Realizing the client is considering military service at the suggestion of his grandfather, a retired military electronics technician who now owns his own business, the Recruiter may likely say to the client, "We can provide you with the same tools that brought success to your grandfather".

That simple statement provokes questions in the client's mind. A part of the client's mind seems to say, "Prove it!" The bold statement is easily recalled later as the client talks with friends and asks for their opinions of the claim.

Throughout your time of presenting your product to the client, they will mentally refer to this bold claim you have made as you started your sales presentation. Make sure it sums your presentation up simply and accurately.

A Logical Presentation Leads To A Purchase

When you join a sales organization, you will be given some sort of product knowledge training. Hopefully, you'll be instructed on all the features and benefits of your product or service. You'll learn to operate it or how to cause it to do whatever it does. The American Salesman is the greatest in the world at gathering information so each sales presentation will be personalized to the exact client they are serving. The concept is to personalize each presentation in such a way that the client will imagine the product or service is already in their possession. They will visualize it in operation in their own personal application. Only at that point can they make a logical and wise decision regarding whether to purchase. Once they reach this mental point, they want the product or service and may even insist on immediate delivery. Quite often, the customer will actually stop you in the midst of your personalized presentation and say, "I'll take it". You never even have to ask them to buy!

Television commercials are entertaining. We all have a favorite. Chances are, your favorite makes its point in an understandable way. Of course, since you're an American, the commercial is entertaining – probably funny. We quickly grasp and remember simple truth. Famous speakers speak in understandable phrases using everyday words.

As you gathered information from the client regarding what they liked and didn't like about their current product or service, you listened and heard two or three needs your product could fill. The decision-maker has just told the most important points to you. Your presentation should consist of those two or three points.

Justify your conversation about each point by referring to the client's own words. "You told me you needed a five-bedroom house, didn't you", the Real Estate professional asks. Then the professional addresses that particular point in order to make sure it supports the bold claim that started the sales presentation.

As the Real Estate professional addresses the selling point that the house has five bedrooms, they refer to the blueprints, pictures or they stand in the center of the house and point out each room. This is a way of offering proof beyond mere words. Clients are naturally skeptical of salespeople's claims. Offering proof eases the mind of the client and helps them focus on their decision rather than on the salesperson's honesty.

In keeping with the concept of simple selling, wise sales professionals constantly check the progress of their presentation. Since the client is the ultimate judge of a sales presentation's progress, they are the one to ask. Each time you make a point with a client, ask an affirming question. When the Real Estate professional asked, "You told me you needed a five-bedroom house, didn't you", they honestly already knew the client had specified a five-bedroom home. Now they're asking the client if that is really important. Or perhaps they're asking if five bedrooms will be enough. The answer to this question will tell us if we're on the right track with a client.

Asking questions that require the client to give an affirmative answer will also aid the client in achieving a positive mindset. Later we're going to ask for a check or purchase order. This small commitment in answering a question during the sales presentation tells us whether the client will likely make the purchase. That's exactly what the answer to the question is - a commitment. If the client will give us small commitments during our presentation, a commitment at the close of the sale will be natural. If, on the other hand, the client says "no" to one of the questions during our presentation, we know the client is easing up on their willingness to commit. We also know exactly where the weak link is in our presentation and we can correct it on the spot.

When I was a little boy in growing up in North Carolina, we had 'Show and Tell' each week at Winfall Elementary School. Each child in Mrs. Tunnel's first grade class would stand up and make a little presentation about some facet of their lives and the rest of us would listen. I always enjoyed a presentation about something the child had obviously enjoyed because the child was animated and exciting. As they told the story, I could imagine being right there as the events took place!

Selling is a lot like 'Show and Tell' since you are on stage as you present your product or service to the client. You need to be interesting and animated as you present the client with their solution. This is a big deal to the client. They will be giving you a lot of money if they decide to purchase. You should be genuinely excited about your product, realizing the client will never be more excited about the product than you are. Watch and listen as you show and tell. What's the client's facial expression? When they reply to your questions, do they sound excited or do they seem bored? In other words, what is your client's body language telling you about the likelihood of a purchase?

An Advertising Sales professional was making a presentation to a soft drink company. The meeting was in the boardroom on the top floor of a tall building in San Antonio. As the board members intently listened, the Ad Rep laid out the details of the largest campaign the company had ever seen. At the end of the presentation, the board voted "no" and the Ad Rep was dismissed from the room as the meeting moved on to other matters. The rejected Ad Rep pressed the elevator button in the hallway, suddenly realizing the omitted information that would have caused the client to accept the proposal. What could he do? Go back in and tell them! Right? No, it was too late.

As you make your sales presentation, your client's feedback is extremely important. During the presentation, you can compensate for any hesitation. Once you ask the obligating question, the sales presentation is over. Hindsight may be 20/20, but in the sales arena hindsight is useless. Get constant feedback from your client as you present your product. Ask questions. Watch the client and listen to the answers. The ability to read the customer is one of the distinguishing characteristics of the American Salesman.

At some point in the presentation, the client's feedback is going to send a message that they are ready to buy. When the client wants the product, help them get it!

How Many Do You Want?

Although my brother is not a salesman, he has a saying that I often apply when asking a client the obligating question. He's the sort of fellow who always has the idea to do something new and creative. Before long, he'll ask a friend or relative to try some new thing. Whenever my brother asks some obligating question he usually gets a positive reply. I once asked him how he could appear so confident all the time when asking such questions and he said, "I see no reason to deny them of what they truly want!" Wow! Talk about a sales principal!

When you ask a client to buy, are you asking them to do what they truly want? Or are you simply asking them to accept your offer? If you're asking a client to do what they truly want to do, they will always say yes! This is the overwhelming reason for asking for feedback during the sales process. This is also the reason to closely read your client's feedback during the sales process. When I see my client beginning to want my product, it is my duty to help them get it. Perhaps this was the origin of the worn out retail phrase, "May I help you?"

You must have figured by now that this sort of selling does not focus on all the powerful ways to 'close the sale'. Closing a well-presented sale is as natural as choosing a spoon rather than a knife for eating your cereal. You don't give it much thought. You simply do it.

Decision Time

At this point in the presentation as the client shows more and more positive feedback, the Military Recruiter might ask, "Do you see what I meant when I said we can provide you with the same tools that brought success to your grandfather?" In asking the client this question the Recruiter is really asking, "Does this make sense? Is it believable?"

With the client's positive response to this question, the next logical question is, "Is this what you had in mind?" Some sales professionals ask, "Can you see this product working out in your situation?" As in the previous question, the client is being asked for an opinion. These are not uncomfortable or obligating questions. But when the client responds favorably to these questions, it's time to help them get the product.

In order for a client to purchase a product or service, they must decide. Your responsibility as a professional salesperson is to help the client make that decision. If you've been working in the sales profession for some time, you already have your own way of asking for a decision. If you're new to the profession you may have not cultivated your own style.

Timing is extremely important since the obligating question can only be logically asked once. Asking the same question over and over gets the same answer over and over, unless your client is intimidated or simply gives in. People who buy in these sorts of situations only buy once and they tell all their friends to avoid that store at all costs.

Sales professionals know that asking for a decision is 'putting it all on the line'. Once you ask a client the obligating question, it's decision time and that takes longer for some clients. Sometimes you may ask a client for a decision and get a 'yes' or 'no' right away. Often, the client will think for a moment or two and then answer. When a client hesitates before answering, wait! Quietly show respect for the client by waiting patiently.

Maintain Silence

Once a professional Real Estate Salesperson told me they called this long pause before a client announced their decision the Abyss of Silence. You're sitting there wondering what the client is thinking and when they will answer. You really want to ask them, "What's going through your mind?" But you know they are simply making a decision and decisions take time. So you sit there in the Abyss of Silence waiting for the client to eventually rescue you.

Occasionally, a salesperson will ask a client for a decision, enter into the Abyss of Silence, and decide they don't like it. They'll begin to talk to the client as the client is trying to make their decision. Have you ever tried to make an important decision with all sorts of interruptions? Not much fun, is it? The more this salesperson talks to the client, the less likely the client will make the best decision.

Some salespeople even start lowering the price while the client is making the decision. Not only are they costing themselves actual commission dollars, they are confusing the client regarding the information necessary for a decision (how much money is this product worth) and further they are creating new questions in the client's mind. Now the client starts wondering if they are actually about to pay too much, since the price seems to be an artificial figure which can change after it seems to be fixed.

Look, Ask, Wait.

I once sold a new truck to a farmer from South Mills North Carolina. The man was in his late 80's, which meant he had endured the Great Depression. He had been a farmer all his life and was very wealthy. But he knew what it took to earn every dollar he had ever touched. When I asked him to write a check for over $20,000 (a relatively low figure for a truck), he sat there and looked at me. I placed the pen near the line on the order form, then quietly sat back in my chair and looked at him. We did this for over five minutes. Five minutes isn't long when you're at the beach or enjoying an evening out with friends. But it's an eternity in a dealership. He never moved or made a sound. Finally, he repeated the figure and asked if that was the best I could do. When I said, "Yes sir." He signed the form and wrote the check. Later he told me he liked me because I didn't put pressure on him.

There is something in all of us that begins to feel uneasy when a conversation ends abruptly. When you've been conversing with a client for over a half hour and you suddenly ask a question and sit in silence, your minds starts saying to you, "Get me out of the Abyss of Silence!"

Don't rob your client of the joy of owning your product simply because you can't be quiet for a few moments and let them process this decision.

Congratulations!

When a customer becomes an owner, they have made a wise decision! They should be congratulated! A professional life-insurance salesman once said to me after I had made a commitment to purchase coverage, "Congratulations on a wise decision, one you'll be very happy with!"

Later, as I was leaving his office, he thanked me for choosing to do business with him.

The client should thank YOU for helping them realizing they needed this product and for helping them get it! Granted, you will be paid a commission. But the client will get the product! Long after your commission is spent, the client will still have the product. The true winner in a sales transaction is the buyer. They get the product! The others only get some money.

America is the land of opportunity. It's also the land of competition. For every great opportunity, there are large numbers of candidates. For every client in the marketplace, there are large numbers of hungry salesmen. The greater the opportunity and the richer the potential in a sales position, the more you will need to offer in order to secure that position. The information in this chapter is essential to a person who intends to succeed in a sales career.

It all boils down to five simple steps;

> Establish Rapport
>
> Gather Information
>
> Confirm The Client's Primary Interest
>
> Personalize The Sales Presentation
>
> Let The Client Decide

Many sales people do not do half the things on these pages, yet they make a comfortable living. If you follow these steps and avoid shortcuts, you will outshine your ill-equipped competition.

CHAPTER FIVE

What To Know Before Your First Sales Call

Stranger Coming!

The rural southern states are sometimes referred to as the Bible belt. Churches dot the landscape and nearly every family is involved in some way with a local church so the name seems appropriate. Some even joke that the most convenient time to burglarize a rural southerner's home is Sunday morning, since he is most likely at Sunday school or church. Even in an age when mega-churches are sweeping the cities of America, in the little communities of the south the Baptists and Methodists, Pentecostals and Episcopalians dress up and head for the little local church house.

In this biblical culture, one group of folks are well known for their zeal as they endeavor to attract people away from Christianity and into their cult. Especially during fair weather, these proselytes will move in groups of two or three through the neighborhoods of their country neighbors and go door-to-door peddling their religion. They open by saying they know something you don't, and before long they're attacking the belief system of the person nice enough to open the door and not sick the dog on them.

For the life of me, I cannot figure out why these people target 'churched' people! Churched people already read the Bible and know the ideas and ideals of this group have been proven incorrect, even dangerous, over and over. Why don't they head to the homes of people who don't go to church? Those folks are open to most anything! While the church folks are defensive from the minute the people with the briefcases and the magazines step onto their property till the proselytes 'shake the dust from their feet' and go to the next house, the eager visitors seem to never get the hint.

On several occasions, I've even seen them knock on a Baptist Preacher's door and try to convert him. He always has compassion on them and interacts with them, challenging their unfounded claims and proving the availability of the true way using scripture. But the mind-numbed robots soon tune him out, shake the dust and head to the next house.

Talk about self-defeating! What a waste of time and effort!

While some may praise the zeal and positive thinking of such prospectors, I'm reminded of prospecting snapshots from the Bible itself. When Jesus sent his 12 disciples out on their first missionary journey and even later when he sent out the larger group of 70, he made a point on both occasions to instruct them to start their prospecting at homes of people already affiliated with them. He further instructed them to invest their time with receptive people. In the Sermon on the Mount, Jesus even said not to cast pearls before swine or give what is holy to the dogs. In other words, the followers of Jesus should pass his message on to those most likely to accept it. In good old southern terms, don't keep running into a brick wall when you see an obvious gate.

It makes great sense that the Lord of all creation would know about selling, since selling is a mental business and He created the mind according to the first chapter of John's Gospel. Wasn't it Jesus who said, "Ask and you'll receive, seek and you'll find, knock and it'll be opened to you"? Sounds like a sales manager, doesn't he!

We in sales often see ourselves as being in the 'persist until they buy' business and our clients in the 'reject and refuse' business. We anticipate and even expect rejection! Back at the sales office, we sometimes recount to our peers the shocking story of a client who bought the product within minutes of the presentation's beginning and never even tried to negotiate! When people want our product, we're amazed!

Actually, your client wants your product more than you want to make the sale! He never would have granted you an appointment or come to your store if he didn't want your product. The only reason a person goes head to head with a salesman is to get a product. Yet we sales professionals often slip into a mode of thinking that convinces us certain people are simply looking or have no intention of buying.

A few people will be eternal shoppers. Even with the assistance of the greatest sales professionals, certain people cannot commit. But that accounts for only a very few. Most people are about getting what they want.

Recall the last time you went shopping for an automobile or truck. How did you feel as you drove onto the lot? Were you a little apprehensive? And when the salesman appeared, did you feel relief because you knew he'd help you get your new vehicle? More likely, you immediately assumed a defensive profile, carefully guarding every word you said for fear he'd take advantage of you.

Why even go to the car lot if you don't trust the salesman? Because you want a new car! And Americans always get what they want.

This situation can be applied to your product or service. Customers naturally distrust salespeople. Our culture has taught us to think that way. Each time you make a presentation to a stranger, the stranger is deciding first of all about you. Once they trust you, then they can focus on your product. If you're calling on people who don't have to experience the 'salesman evaluation' step, you'll obviously sell more.

Perhaps you are beginning to realize the importance of carefully choosing which clients you spend your time calling on.

Call on Friendly Clients

A Wildlife Officer once told me deadly poisonous snakes and some large wild animals capable of hurting and even killing a human are actually not on the hunt for people at all. They are not the least concerned with you until you threaten them. Once threatened, they come at you with lethal force!

Clients are a lot like wildlife in this respect, aren't they? They simply want their product or service. If dealing with you is part of what they must do in order to get what they want, that's just part of the process. They have no opinion of you, good or bad. Until you say or do something that threatens them. Then they charge at you with all sorts of reasons not to buy.

If you're just starting out in the sales business, chances are you've been given a list of places to go and people to see. If you work in a fixed location and customers come to you, you may be seeing lots of strange faces. We all must start somewhere and the first days of selling are always like this. Some companies want you to start with your family and friends, but even in those cases you soon realize you need to cultivate your own clientele.

As you call on clients, you will discover some of them are more receptive to you. Calling on these people is more fun! While professional sales people should be careful not to cross the line and become too familiar with customers, it's still tempting to make more sales calls on the people who are nice to you and who readily buy from you than on the apprehensive rude people.

Actually, calling on receptive clients is psychologically sound! Your sales manager may require you to call on certain accounts where you know you'll be treated badly. Since the sales manager is the boss, you need to call on every account you're instructed to call upon. And you need to succeed in each call. One sure way to keep a successful attitude is to mix as many friendly clients as possible in with the others. This way, each time some client puts you through the wringer before buying; you can then go call on a client who will be glad to see you!

Additionally, you can close more sales with friendly clients than with apprehensive clients. And friendly clients are more candid, enabling you to do a more thorough job of customizing your presentations. Further, friendly clients trust you to be fair with them so time-consuming negotiation is almost absent from the sales process with them.

Follow The Money Trail

Which of the clients you're currently doing business with now is your biggest spender? Which of the clients you've done business with in the past has given you the largest order since you were in sales? This is where you should be spending your time.

Selling real estate taught me this lesson; the same question gets an earnest money contract on a $50,000.00 house or on a $500,000.00 house. And it takes about the same amount of time to build the case for asking that committing question. But one answer nets you 10 times the income!

Big clients are sometimes intimidating with their flamboyant outcroppings. But they want and need your product just as much as the little client who only buys a fraction of the big order.

Since the whole sales world knows the big clients have such deep pockets, these clients become accustomed to being taken advantage of by sales people so they are sometimes difficult to close on the first order or two if they don't know you. But once you are established as a professional whose mind is on business, who has their best interest at heart, they will buy every beneficial product you're selling. Their decision-making process is often much faster than small clients, since one of their success factors is effective time management. And they always buy during off seasons and in poor economic times, while small operators scale down.

One lesson you learn from pursuing big accounts and powerful clients is to sell service rather than price. Although some clients may occasionally tell you "money is no object", all clients are concerned to some extent with price. But most clients are not obsessed with how much something costs. What they really want to know is what they get for the money and what the product or service will do for them.

"Two for the price of one" is less about the 'price' and more about the 'two'. The lowest price in the world, on a product of no value, is no bargain. The greatest product in the world, at any price, is a great value. Yet sales people chase price far too often when they should be building value.

If you are face to face with your client, and that client has done business with you over and over, they already know they are paying a little extra for the service and dependability you bring to the table. Read this sentence carefully – the client's perception of your excellent customer service and dependability is earned, not talked about. Telling a client you are dependable and you will provide good service is a waste of breath since all your competitors say that about themselves already. These words go in one ear and out the other. The proof is in the track record.

Clients can acquire your product or service from several sources, including the Internet. The reason they're buying from you is they place value on your role in the process. And they know they are paying extra for it. So leave price out of discussions with faithful clients unless the client brings it up. They don't keep doing business with you so you can discuss price. They continue to do business with you so they can get the best product and so they'll have quick access to you if a supply or service question comes up.

If Not Me, Who? And Why?

Occasionally you'll call on a client who will tell you they aren't interested because they already do business with another firm. Sometimes they'll tell you this after a 30-minute presentation! Rather than stealing away into the night, find out why they choose to do business with that other company. They obviously feel that company solves a problem or fills a need that your company cannot. And they granted you an interview in the hope that you could do some thing or provide some service that competitor is not at this time.

Carefully listen as your client relates why they currently do business with your competitor. In a pleasant way, ask "If you could change one thing about the product or your relationship with the competitor, what would that be?" You'll soon find yourself hearing exactly what the client wishes the competitor would do. Remember, if the competitor is solving all the problems and providing excellent service, the client will send you on your way in short order without listening to your presentation. The longer they talk with you, the more interested they are in your product and the more they need your service.

Once you determine what it will take to earn the client's business, ask yourself if you and your product can handle that order. If the answer is yes, present the solution to the client and ask for his business as though the competitor does not exist.

Avoid getting into a price war with the competition. Often a client, who is satisfied with his current supplier and has no intention of changing, will shop with other companies in order to beat down the current supplier's price. By the way, in most cases this indicates the supplier is not spending enough time building the client's trust through good account service. If you win a price war with a competitor, the victory will be short lived. Sooner or later, someone else is going to cut your price and you will be out. There is always a cheaper product available. But there is not always a better product or more customer-oriented sales professional. Service trumps price every time!

Sales professionals who create desire to own their products, by showing how it will solve problems and fill needs, will always have customers. On the other hand, companies with the lowest price will only have customers when times are good and people are already buying.

How Much Product Knowledge Is Enough?

If your client is buying from you because they perceive you are valuable in a service situation, it serves to reason you should know the service details of your product.

The 1994 product year was a great one for GM trucks. Due to a surge in front-wheel-drive automobiles with V-6 engines, Americans in the 40 to 60 year age group who were used to driving rear-wheel-drive V-8 cars were starting to drive dressed up pickup trucks. These people knew the long standing excellent reputation of the 350 engines so GM trucks were moving off the lots as fast as dealers could get them.

One evening, a retirement-aged gentleman that I knew from church came in and bought a new truck. The comfortable transaction took less than an hour and he drove away smiling.

That night he called me at home and wanted me to immediately come to his house so he could show me something. We solemnly walked to the garage and he started he truck, pointing to the oil pressure gauge, which read 10 psi. Having owned several GM trucks equipped with 350 V-8 engines, he insisted the truck was faulty. We looked at the Owner's Manual and discovered this was normal. Now he really didn't want the truck. How could a 350 operate at freeway speeds pulling his camper if it had such low oil pressure?

His concern was based on experience. Since 1968, the GM 350 V-8 would usually hold around 20 psi oil pressure at idol and as much as 80 psi at highway speeds. He routinely observed many of his former trucks performing this way for years. Tonight he noticed his oil pressure never got over 50 on the way home. This has to be a bad engine!

The next morning, the service manager and one of the mechanics that owned a racecar equipped with a 350 V-8 explained why General Motors had changed the technology of the engine to perform better with a lower oil pressure. They cited reports and statistics and referred to the shop manual. After two hours, the gentleman came back to my office and said he was going to keep the truck but he didn't trust it on the road.

Some weeks later, the gentleman came in one afternoon and politely asked for a moment of my time. This man is a NASCAR fan so he reads all the information about what's going on in NASCAR. He explained certain engines had problems with too much oil pressure causing damage to the engine at high speeds. Now he was confident his new truck was equipped with the very best 350 V-8 he had ever owned.

Suppose I had included the oil pressure information in my initial sales presentation to the client? Trouble is, I didn't know about the new oil pressure or why it was reduced. You can rest assured; I made sure future mature buyers of trucks with 350 engines knew about the new oil pressure technology and its advantage to them.

While car salesmen are not the best people to work on cars, they are the first people that come to the minds of car owners when something malfunctions. "I bought this thing from you and now it doesn't work right! I expect you to make this problem go away!"

It's the same if you're selling office equipment or health insurance or agricultural supplies. Clients do business with you in part so they will have an insider if something goes wrong with the product at some point.

Your sales manager is certainly going to require you to learn all about your product. Do you know how the product was made? Do you know the procedures for service on the product or what is abnormal in its operation? Do you know how long certain maintenance or service operations require the product to be in the shop? The customer sees you as the contact point for all things having to do with the product. You need to know everything there is to know about your product, even things you aren't required to know about functions you would never attempt to do. You are the expert in your client's eyes. Earn the title!

What Do I Need To Know About The Competition?

When General Motors changed the style of their S-series trucks from the square style of the 1980's to a more updated sleek style in the early 1990's, they trained all the sales professionals who sold their trucks on the features and benefits of the new S-series trucks. At locations all over the country, sales professionals spent half a day in class and the remainder of the day driving on a closed course. It was truly a most beneficial day of learning for them.

In the classroom, every feature and benefit of the new GM truck was examined and explained. In addition, GM sales professionals learned the features and benefits of the new Toyota and Ford Ranger pickups.

Once the driving started, sales professionals drove the new GM truck then drove the Toyota and the Ranger. If these sales professionals sold GM trucks, why did they need to waste time driving or discussing Toyota and Ford?

You're ahead of me. Because Toyota and Ford were interested in selling trucks to the same prospects GM was interested in selling to. When your customer says, "I want to check out the competition", he is sometimes saying, "I want to make sure this is the best application for my situation." How can you possibly know the answer to that question if the only product you have mastered is your own?

Great sales professionals always learn everything there is to know about the competition's product. You should know enough about your competition's product that you could sell it yourself. You should know why your product is better than the competition and also what the competition's product can do that your product cannot do. If all you know about the competition's product is negative, head back to the drawing board for the rest of the story. By the way, sooner or later the competition's sales manger is probably going to give you the opportunity to sell their product!

Some great sales professionals even learn how the competition's sales force functions and what bonus programs they enjoy. Sometimes a client reacts in an interesting manner if they discover a particular product they are considering buying from the competition carries a $1000.00 bonus for the salesman.

Before you ever decide to sell a product or service, you need to ask yourself if it is the very best available. At some point, this question will come straight at you from your client. As you make sales presentations to clients, they'll pick up on little things you say or the way you say them. These little comments will tell the tale about your true feelings regarding your product or service. Your client will seldom be more enthused about your product than you are, even when they buy. Before you take a position with a company representing a particular product, make sure you are confident about the product and sold on it yourself. Selling an inferior product successfully is almost impossible, and it is always very frustrating. Stick with a line you believe in and can be proud of!

Beware Being Driven Like The Competition

Reactionary selling occurs when competitors become obsessed with each other to the point that they focus their energy on constantly trying to one-up each other. Salespeople sometimes do this do this too. It may even happen between two members of the same sales team. Whether the competition is between salespeople or companies, both competitors always lose. Great sales professionals come to realize that you are only in competition with yourself and what you did last week or last year. The minute you begin to focus on beating the competition, you take your eyes off serving the client.

Consider how most Americans react to political ads. If it's true that successful television advertising is written for understanding at the third grade level, then third graders themselves must write political ads. Wait! I know some third graders who are way too smart and too mature to write such vindictive tripe! You'd think the leaders of our culture would have more dignity than to resort to this classless display. Yet the mudslinging childishness occurs every election season, at every level.

When you get into a price war with the competition as you both give away the store in order to buy business away form each other, the clients may take advantage of your low price but they will not likely build a customer-for-life relationship with you. And they will come to view your product as artificially over priced.

100 Shoppers - How Many Buyers?

One reaction to a temporary lull in the marketplace is often placing advertising. For several years I made a good living selling advertising so you need to know that I believe in it. Every business needs to advertise but they need to advertise strategically.

When 100 people come to your place of business because they saw or heard an ad, it's usually because they have been exposed to information about your business a minimum of 16 times. Keep that in mind if you are the person buying the ads. If you cannot purchase enough ads for a frequency of advertising that guarantees a minimum of 16 powerful exposures to your message, you may as well not advertise.

On the average, less than 20 of those 100 people coming to your place of business responding to an ad will buy. All 100 require the attention of the sales staff. If you are happy closing less than 20 % of the clients you serve, this ought to get you excited.

Some of the people who come to your place of business during normal operations, or during an ad blitz, will spend time with the sales staff but will need to think it over or will put off the decision to buy for some other reason. Sometimes sales professionals will keep in touch with these clients, calling them or emailing them whenever they have new information that was not covered the day the client visited the business. If a client returns to your business because you have kept in touch with them after their initial visit, over 50% of those will buy. So if 100 people come in, shop, leave, and you keep in touch until they come back to the store, you will close over half of those deals.

Everybody prefers to have a contact at a place of business when they shop there. If your friend has told you about a special sale on the exact model of boat you've been looking for and has told you the name of a friend of theirs who is on the sales staff, you've probably felt a lot more confident as you entered the store and went right to that person. Each time you close a sale with a client, you should give them the opportunity to do this excellent service for their friends. When you ask for a referral at the moment of closing a sale, your customer will likely give you a genuine lead. When you contact that person who was referred to you and mention that the friend said you should call, your rapport with the client is already on the fast track. When 100 referred clients visit your store and deal with you personally, almost two thirds of them will buy! All because you asked for a referral and took the time to call or email the client and follow up.

The group of clients who will buy at a higher rate – almost three fourths – are the clients with whom you have previously done business. When you stay in touch with your customers after they purchase until the next time they purchase, over 70% who shop with you will buy. So when you spend time with 4 clients, 3 will buy! Does that sound like your closing ratio?

By the way, what does this say about how sales professionals should work their clients? And which clients should they spend the bulk of their time pursuing? Sort of shoots the idea of standing around the store waiting for people to show up in the head!

Be An Early Bird

The early bird gets the worm! How old were you when you first heard that wise saying? It's still very true, especially in the sales business.

Customers make their best decisions early in the day. And they make them faster, leaving you plenty of time to see other clients! With a clear head and a clear desk, the buyer will deal with you from a fresh perspective. The more sales calls you can make before noon, the more you will sell. If you are in a fixed business location, make every effort to work by appointment. And make those appointments early in the day.

Along with casual Friday comes early departure Friday. Some even depart on Thursday evening during fair weather or near holidays. So you should arrange client contacts early in the week as well. Appointments set for Monday through Wednesday typically net better results than those on Thursday or Friday. When follow-up calls are necessary, the early-in-the-week appointment can be followed up on Thursday or Friday. The Thursday or Friday call will need to be followed up next week, following the weekend when the mind sometimes takes a vacation.

Early in the month, the client's mind is optimistic about the month ahead. During the first 8 to 10 days of the month, decisions are made with a clear and positive mindset. If the client encounters challenges that seem overwhelming and need to be handled before the end of the month, those last 10 days turn into obsession.

Some companies have a professional buyer who deals with you. Like you, this buyer is dealing with a set figure that must be met. The buyer needs to handle all the business for the quarter early in the quarter since unexpected events take place that bog the buyer down in paperwork or endless searches for a service or product. If you sell to a professional buyer, call on the buyer during the first 3 to 5 days of the new quarter. Once you establish a pattern with the buyer and become a trusted supplier, they will tell you if another time is better.

One thing I remember about selling advertisement is that merchants typically operated on an annual budget. Advertising was one of the line items. So there you had the year's advertising budget all laid out. If I could determine my client's annual ad budget and bring a proposal for what that budget could do for the client on a month-to-month basis, an annual contract was a shoe-in. The easier you make it for a client to do business with you, the more they will.

Avoid The Last Minute Rush

By the way, your own month will go better if you make every effort to reach your sales goal by the 20th rather than by the last day. In all my years as a sales manager, I was amazed by the sales people who were excellent at convincing clients of the value of long-range planning and early decisions yet who waited till the last day or two of the month to make their goal. Maybe you know someone who likes to live like this. Hope it isn't you!

Make it a habit to track yourself in order to know where you are in terms of your sales goal. Break your monthly goal down to weekly and daily goals. Determine how many clients you need to visit with in order to close one sale. If your goal is financial, determine how many sales you need to make in order to reach that figure. When you break the figure down to a daily figure, be sure to put as much of the load in the first 3 days of the week as possible. Also set your sights on the first 3 weeks of the month. Sales professionals close so many more sales with so much less effort when they are not under the gun of making quota!

Keep a personal sales journal and make daily entries. Did you read the word 'personal'? This is not something for the company higher-ups to look at; it's your personal tool to move you closer to your goal. If you know that doing certain things or calling on certain clients causes you to close more sales, those are the things you should do over and over.

In your journal, note daily where you should be in relation to your goal for the month and where you actually are. The sales business is an up and down business. If you see your progress on paper, the hills and valleys begin to even out. You won't give up just because you have 3 bad days in a row if you see you are still on track for the month. By the same token, you won't start thinking you no longer need to work this month after you close a big fat sale, if you see you still need a little more to make the boss happy.

The very best sales management is self-management. If your boss is a strong sales manager they will echo this!

Always Collect The Money

If you're on commission, your check is figured on collected funds. Your sales contests are based on closed and collected deals. Notice the recurrence of the word 'collected'!

Bringing a check in with a contract assures you will get a check for your work. The reverse is also true. Just as the commission on "I'll think about it" is zero, the commission on a contract without a check is zero.

Bringing a check in with a contract also helps your client. The company is motivated to expedite delivery and put their best foot forward when the client has paid up front. The client who pays will not have to worry about handling payment in the future. It's done! Just ask anyone whose home is paid for!

If you can ask for the order, asking for the check is a normal part of the process. Your client is expecting to give you money if you give them services. Never assume the order is too big for a check.

When you call on the client for the next order, the previous order is paid off and clear. This puts the client in a positive frame of mind. If the client still owes you for last month, that fact could cause them to decide not to buy today.

If a client becomes a slow or late paying customer, this is a signal you need to slide a new source of income into the mental budget slot you have that client in. Continue to give the slow paying client the same outstanding service you always did! Do not penalize your reputation as an outstanding professional just because your client will not pay or is experiencing a bad time.

Clients who don't know how to manage money well go through times like this often but they always seem to continue to hang on. Many businesses have slow times when their clients do not pay, causing them to suffer low cash flow. Later when things get better, they will reward you for your faithfulness and consistency while your competition turned their backs on them.

If you replace the slow paying client with a good paying client, your commissions will continue to flow and you will not suffer the shortfall of cash that comes when a contract does not fund or a bill is not paid. Successful sales professionals are responsible people who plan ahead and take responsibility for their financial needs and wants rather than falling behind and blaming clients who cannot or do not pay.

Time Is Money

If you are one of the lucky Americans who are married, you have a special reason to go home each night! And if you have been blessed with some children, that reason is multiplied!

We go to work to get money for our families. That's the reason we work. We all talk at some point about playing. Young people talk about the weekend. Middle-aged folks look forward to vacation. And some of us look forward to retirement! No phone, no job, no boss! You've seen the bumper sticker.

Since the real reason for working is those loved ones at home, make sure all your time away from them counts. Manage your sales career like the vital gift it is. Make every minute count. If you commit yourself to making every minute of time in a day of selling count, you will probably take a little heat for working too hard. But when you go home, you can leave the job at the office, knowing you gave it your all and also knowing the bills are paid.

CHAPTER SIX

My Real Estate Professional Knows

To Dream The Impossible Dream

Home ownership represents a big part of the American Dream. There is something liberating about being one's own landlord and personalizing your property. But I learned the hard way that you need an insider if you're a young uninformed couple who wants to own a home.

In 1971, I was transferred to Richmond Virginia as an Air Force Recruiter. We were excited since Richmond was less than a three-hour drive from Chowan County North Carolina where my wife's parents and all her relatives lived. The aroma of tobacco was in the Richmond air early every morning and the big city feel was intoxicating to a couple of country kids. Lots of stores carried every product you could ever want or need. Living in Richmond was going to be great! We couldn't wait to go house shopping.

Prior to the stripping of the military manning in the 1990's, the Air Force would give you a week or so to take care of getting settled in at a new duty station. That included shopping for and moving into a new home. We decided to stay with her parents in North Carolina and make the commute each day as we shopped for the Dannelly mansion. Back in Texas, I had attended a briefing about military benefits and they explained that a VA loan was the best way to buy a home. There was no down payment, certain construction standards had to be met and the interest rate was always competitive. Such a deal! No down payment! And the VA Loan was good for up to $12,500.00! That's the bulk of what I heard.

Living in north Texas near Sheppard Air Force Base, we had seen several nice houses for $10,000.00 to $12,000.00 and had decided it was time to own a home. Reality was about to set in. In 1971, far fewer people were in the Real Estate business in Richmond. Most of those were what I refer to as 'also' Real Estate companies. They sold insurance, securities and 'also' real estate. The anti-military atmosphere was present everywhere we went and nobody had heard of a VA Loan.

Being the helpful green salesman and really wanting a home for my little bride, I explained to the nice folks at each company how the VA Loan worked. That down-payment thing always really threw them since they were accustomed to getting around 20 percent down, and they liked to see that money before any shopping took place. But I used eye contact, persisted and was convincing. So the first sales person took us out to look at some $12,000.00 homes. Even though it was 1971, it was a shocking experience. The $12,000.00 home was a dump! And not even a dump with potential!

We looked at house after house. The sales person would take us to the house, apologetically ask the residents if we could interrupt them, then the sales person would step aside and let us 'endure' the property. I think we looked at 8 or 10 properties, most of them occupied, all of them nasty and in poor repair. Several tenants expressed their disapproval of the military and the war we baby-killers had started in Vietnam. At the end of the day, my wife asked for the sales person's card and told them we needed to go home and think about it. Have you ever driven 3 hours without speaking?

When we got to her parents beautiful home in the country, she ran upstairs to her old room, laid across the bed and cried. I wanted to pack up everything and go back to being an instructor at Sheppard Air Force Base and working for Frank at the Western Auto Store. Life was so simple there and people liked military folks! And the Real Estate people would actually let you buy a house! But that was not reality. I had worked hard to be selected for Recruiting duty and over a third of the students in my class at Air Force Recruiting School had washed out. We were meant to be in Richmond so it was my duty to make it all work. Time to do some thinking and problem solving.

Problem Solving

What we needed was a less confrontational experience. Since most people in Richmond seemed to have a serious problem with people in uniform, I decided to wear civilian clothes. We needed a dedicated Real Estate professional, not somebody who did it part time or on the side. And we needed to figure a way to get my father-in-law to lend us about $10,000.00 since it appeared the nice homes in Richmond were in the $20,000.00 range.

Just like they taught me in NCO Academy, I had defined the problem. So here we went again. Civilian clothes – check! I had a Richmond phone book and circled 3 dedicated Real Estate companies. Dedicated Real Estate professional – check! At breakfast, I used eye contact, sincere genuine verbiage and discussed my financial idea with my father-in-law. North Carolina farmers tend to be extremely conservative. This comes from all the years when they have barely scraped by or even lost money and had to sell this or that in order to keep afloat. He was having a streak of good years, but like Joseph in Egypt, he knew all years are not good. He also knew he wouldn't be doing his little girl and her husband any favors if he handed it to us on a silver platter. Father-in-law loan – no check! I still believed 2 out of 3 was a good average so we headed to Richmond for yet another day of brain damage.

Specializing In REAL Estate Sales

The dedicated Real Estate company was fun! They liked us since we were driving a new Chevrolet and were dressed like we were going to church. They told us we would like Richmond and its entire historic flavor. Everything was going great until I told them we were shopping for a home in the $12,000.00 range and wanted to finance it with a VA Loan.

Brick wall! Suddenly the friendly lady became cold and distant. She did her best to convince us to rent an apartment from them. But I wasn't defeated.

We got back into the car and headed to the next Real Estate Store. My wife told me to go in and hit them with the facts and come back out to the car and fetch her, only if they didn't freak out. She was wise. They freaked out. VA Loan? $12000.00 house? I was so thankful I didn't tell them I was active duty military! It was a 1-minute interview.

We had one more place to stop before we went back down to Chowan County North Carolina and humbly asked my father-in-law if we could live in my wife's old room. Since it was around noon, we went to a little restaurant and brainstormed as we ate. We started accepting the fact that Richmond was not the place to live. We knew we could find a place around Chowan County North Carolina but that would mean a daily 6-hour commute. It's amazing how you solve problems when you're frustrated and young!

We drove up to the last Real Estate company on the list. My wife decided to be a good sport and go in with me. We had to wait for almost an hour for the fellow who would be working with us. He was out showing a property. When he came in, I decided to interact with him a little before I hit him with the facts. He was very polished and professional. Before I knew it, he was asking us about our likes and dislikes in a new home. I regained my composure and hit him with the facts. VA Loan! $12,000.00 house!

Education Of The Buyer

He never even blinked.

"Why are you limiting yourself to a $12,000.00 house" he asked, "your VA entitlement goes much higher than that." I was 'all ears'. He explained that the VA was really only a guarantee against a loan from a bank or mortgage company and that the guarantee was 4 times the figure! According to the financial information he had obtained from us, we could afford a nice home. And homes meeting VA standards were nicer than most. We were elated! We had found a Real Estate professional! He could help us get our own house!

We sat for over an hour discussing what we wanted in a house. He asked us what we didn't want to experience in a house as well! We talked about school districts and where my office would be. He asked my wife where she liked to do her shopping and where we planned to go to church. He asked us how much we'd be comfortable paying each month, including our taxes and insurance on the home. Then he looked at us as though he had suddenly had some sort of thought and said, "I know just the house. You'll love it! Would you like to go take a look at it?" With our hearts in our throats, we said yes! We got into his luxury automobile and off we went.

He turned into a nice conservative neighborhood about a mile from Richmond's only shopping mall and drove up in front of a beautiful brand new home. The yard wasn't even landscaped yet! He unlocked the front door and we looked around the place for a minute. Then he started in the living room and pointed out every feature we had just told him we wanted back in his office. He kept referring to his copy of the contract on that home as he informed us about it. When I asked if the house had air conditioning, he asked me, "Do you want air conditioning?" My wife said we did and he wrote on the contract, "Include air conditioner on note."

After about half an hour, he looked at us and said, "Is this your house?" She spoke for both of us. "Yes!"

Make It Easy To Do Business

We were fortunate because he whisked us right over to the bank for the loan application. The bank was also very knowledgeable of the VA Loan process. In addition, they welcomed me to Richmond as the new Air

Force Recruiter. After that, our Real Estate professional drove us past our new home one more time and back to his office. In the parking lot, he thanked us for allowing him to serve us and told us he'd call us the next day to let us know about closing and the official move-in date.

Perhaps you've lived an experience like this one. We were not difficult clients! We were simply different from the norm. What a joy for us to find an inside contact that could help us get a house!

I'm glad we met this man. For starters, he knew his business, including the law. Not only did he know what a VA Loan was, he knew all the details of it. He knew the qualifications for that transaction included strict construction details. And he was prepared to only show us properties that would easily pass the VA inspection.

Among the topics we discussed in his office before going out to look at the house of our dreams, he asked how long we planned to live in Richmond. The Air Force had told me 3 to 4 years. He suggested we needed to plan for a home that would increase in value and be attractive to a buyer in 3 years. He suggested it needed to be in a good school district, though we didn't have children, and near shopping centers and grocery stores. And the neighborhood needed to display a pride of ownership. Here I was simply thinking of buying a house and he was helping me get it ready to sell.

He made the entire process easy. He was with us right down to the day we signed the paperwork. We never encountered a single problem he couldn't handle. Closing couldn't take place for another month and we needed a place to live now. He negotiated an arrangement for us to rent the house for that month. The day we moved in, he stopped by for a few minutes just to make sure we had everything we needed and to make sure I knew where the hardware stores and lawn and garden stores were.

By the way, we paid a little under $18000 for the house. And it was financed with a VA guarantee on the loan from a local bank.

Do you realize the value of your service as a professional Real Estate Salesperson? It's far more than the few thousand dollars you are paid to sell a property.

Aggressive Listing Results In Sold Properties

One fact that escapes many people is that the profession of Real Estate Sales is all about selling. Certainly, if you show a property to a client and they purchase the property, you are selling. But when you list a property for sale, you're also selling. And you're selling more than the owner who must sign the listing agreement.

Real property that is correctly listed will sell. Beyond the obvious, correct price and information correctly documented, is the not-so-obvious question, "Who's the customer?" "Who is it we need to market this house to?"

The prime customer for any home you list for sale is the local Real Estate professional.

Each committed real estate professional is currently in touch with at least twenty clients. Some Real Estate sales professionals have an ongoing relationship with many more than twenty! If the property is effectively marketed to the general public, chances are a few people will be interested. If the property is effectively marked to ONE Real Estate professional, at least twenty clients will hear about it and some may be shown the property right away. Now multiply that by the total number of Real Estate Agents working your market. Where are you marketing your listings?

As a Real Estate professional, why would you show a property listed by another agent? After all, if you list AND sell a property, you split the entire commission with your broker. On the other hand, if you see that a property listed by another agent pays 2 percent higher commission, the motivation is clearly there to sell that property! Your income from that transaction is almost as much as the income from selling your own listing! And you only encounter half the work!

Real Estate sales professionals are practical people. They realize the selling agent must be enticed if the client is to ever see the property. One means of enticing agents is financial. The most obvious financial avenue is the sales commission, set at the time of listing the property for sale.

All sorts of taboos surround the magic number of percentage points of the selling price designated for sales commission. Although almost every state in the union has discouraged fixing the sales commission, a particular number seems to end up on most listing agreements. Whatever that number is, add 2 percentage points to your listings. On a $100,000.00 listing that represents $2,000.00.

If your client has been exposed to one of the $500.00 listing plans or it's cousin, the 'one percentage point under everyone else' plan, be prepared to do some educating. While Americans sometimes feel the lowest bid is the one to take, your client needs to understand they are hiring a selling agent away from every other property owner in the market whose home is on the market. Some of these property owners are in better school districts or are closer to the prospective buyer's workplace, or a thousand other factors over which your client has no control. One thing your listing client can control is what the selling agent will be paid.

Something in the being of a Real Estate sales professional causes them to look at the sales commission figure on a listing when they see that listing for the first time. Back in the day of the big thick Listing book, I recall how all of us would open it to the new listings and look at the commission figure on the listing. Most of them were the 'particular figure' we were used to seeing. Occasionally, someone would list at 8% or even 10%. You can bet we made sure to go and look at that property! The whole time you were on the Real Estate Agent walk-through, you searched your mind for a prospect among your clients.

Invest In The Desired Result

Education point one for your listing client then is, "Money Talks!"
And it doesn't take much money to talk to the professionals in your
market. Adding $2,000.00 to the selling expense of a $100,000.00
listing gives it immediate preference in the mind of a person who is
paid for their time. By the way, what does the 4% listing say to the
same agent? "Don't kill yourself selling this house! We're not going to
go broke paying you!"

Years ago, when the average selling price of a new home was in the
$50,000.00 range, the commission to the selling agent was around
$1,500.00. Of course the agent split this with their broker so the
bottom line was $750.00. One new homebuilder in the San Antonio
market used to sometimes offer a $1,000.00 bonus to the selling agent.
You'd take your client out to the site office, then walk along with the
site salesperson as they made their 30-minute presentation and closed
the deal. The contract was written right in their office. Then you took
your client back to your office and they were on to the next activity of
the day. Your buyer had found their home and you still had plenty of
time to serve other clients! And you had made more than double the
usual commission!

During months when the market was slow, as it was when interest rates
for new homes went over 16%, the homebuilder would offer Real Estate
sales professionals a $1,000.00 bonus on the first home, $2,500.00 on
the second home and $5000.00 on the third and all other homes your
clients bought from them during a particular weekend. Your wheels
are turning, aren't they!

Plan B - If It Doesn't Sell

Education point two for your listing client then is, "A Little Money
Goes A Long Way!"

If your client has listed their home with you at the nice round figure of $100,000.00 and the market seems to justify this figure prior to the appraisal, what's the normal reaction when 60 days go by and no offers come? If your clients are like most of mine, they want you to run more ads! Or hold an open house!

The longer you spend in the Real Estate profession, the more convinced you would become that an open house seldom sells THAT house. It brings clients interested in lesser houses of that style or other houses on the market in that neighborhood. More likely, it brings curious neighbors in to find out what the asking price is and what sort of furnishings your client has.

The next suggestion by the client is almost always, "Lower the price to $95,000.00!" That is not a good idea, for two reasons. First, when buyers detect a descending price or 'must sell' attitude, offers will be low and the seller will not be in an advantageous position during negotiations. Second, the commission will now be based upon no more than $95,000.00, meaning you have just lost hundreds of your personal income dollars. If a home is worth $100,000.00, lowering the price below market value also causes the client to think something is wrong with the property.

What's the best method of generating activity? If higher than usual sales commissions and if bonuses draw the attention of agents working with twenty or more clients, your client would be better off to increase the percentage of sales commission or the bonus amount.

If your client needs to move quickly, a $5,000.00 bonus to the selling agent will result in a lot more activity than lowering the price $10,000.00. Of course, you need to make sure every agent in your area is aware of the opportunity to knock a home run! Remember this the next time you start lowering the price of your listings. Listing prices should only go up.

CHAPTER SEVEN

How I Chose My Car Sales Professional

My First Dip With The Sharks

Like it or not, a war has gone on between car salesmen and car customers. I'm not sure when this war started since I wasn't introduced to the car business until about 1961 when I first remember going along with my dad as he shopped for something to replace our 1955 Desoto. I remember the dealer in Elizabeth City North Carolina would let my dad take different cars home overnight and that every car seemed to have a particular smell. I also remember my dad going over to the bank and borrowing the money to buy the new 1962 Plymouth Valiant.

In 1965 when I bought my first car from a dealer, I learned the difference in the respect a 52-year old man gets and the treatment a 19-year old mechanic/college student gets on a car lot. I never was allowed to test drive any car. One place I visited told me to come back when my daddy was with me. When I finally found the 1964 Dodge I couldn't live without because of that big V-8 and manual transmission, the salesman told me how much money I'd need to bring back if I wanted to drive the car.

Make A Lasting Impression

The bank was different. When I went in, the loan officer who had done business with my dad remembered me and talked with me for a while about my job at the lumber mill where I maintained log trucks. We discussed my aspirations about becoming an auto mechanic after college. He explained the importance of making timely payments and the value of a paid-off car note when I came to him later to borrow money for a home. Then he whirled around and typed my name on a note and wrote a check to the dealer. The whole process took less than an hour.

I walked back down the street to the dealership where the salesman was showing my car to another customer. After making me wait for almost half an hour while the customer went riding with him in my car, he returned and asked me how it was going. I gave him the check and told him I wanted my car before anybody else took it out joyriding. He chuckled and told me he'd need a couple of hours to get it washed and do the paperwork. Since he told me the paperwork would only take about half an hour, we agreed on his just doing the paperwork and letting me take care of the washing.

That was one of the happiest days in my life. I think I used an entire tank of gas that night showing it off to my friends. But a few weeks later as I drove past the dealership and saw the salesman holding the door open for a young couple, I made the decision that I needed to be more assertive in the future when dealing with car salesmen.

The bank officer made such an impression on me I paid the 2 year note off in a little over 6 months. The car salesman made such an impression on me that I gave car salesmen gray hair for years.

Us Against Them

When I entered the car sales business and started learning their 'ways', I could see why that business had been so confrontational. Terms like "bust the customer" and "turn the customer over" and "lay the customer away" were common talk. The goal was to "slam-dunk" the customer by "loading him up" in the F&I office.

When you met a customer on the lot, your job was to get his name and his car keys as soon as possible. The keys to the car the customer drove on the lot were given to the manager and the only way the customer could get their keys back was to buy a new car.

Car salesmen were taught to ask the customer a question and run tell the manager the customer's reply. With some customers this process could go on for hours. If you were observed thinking or acting on your own, sharp reprimands were given to you from the Drill Sergeant type sales manager. All day long, you ran back and forth parroting what the manager said and reporting what the customer said.

The manager was mad at you because your customer wouldn't pay window sticker and the customer was mad at you because your manager wouldn't give them the car for nothing. By and by, the customer sometimes got mad and stomped out, only to come back in and ask for their keys. You know the rest of that story. "Have a seat in my office and I'll go ask the manager for them."

When you closed a deal, you never knew how much profit your commission was based on, since the procedure demanded the salesman had to be kept in the dark regarding figures. One other important note, most car salesmen lasted at a dealership for about 90 days.

It's a miracle anybody has lasted in the car dealerships operated this way. This is not sales, this is brain damage!

Car-Buying Ought To Be Easy

Saturn saw how tired Americans were of the confrontational car-buying experience when they introduced one-price window stickers in the early 1990's. When other manufacturers tried to follow suit, it didn't work because too many managers and salespeople were stuck in the old ways of confrontational selling.

Americans love their vehicles. They pay dearly for them, personalize them, pamper them and sometimes cry when they trade them off. So it makes sense that selling cars should be extremely profitable and lots of fun. And it was for me, once I quit running back and forth to the man in the prison booth and started 'selling cars'.

When I told my Drill Sergeant and his boss, the Supreme Commander, that I wanted to approach selling this way, they told me to shape up or ship out. I shipped out to a place where customers were appreciated and salesmen were allowed to truly sell. At our dealership, salespeople did the negotiating with customers. Customers kept their keys and nobody got "busted" or "laid away". It was all about people and cars!

I must admit I learned a lot of car sales techniques long before I ever entered the car business. My truck salesman in San Antonio was a man who loved people and loved selling trucks. He came by my office every few months and talked with me about how the needs of my business were changing. Almost every time he came by, I soon ended up with another truck. He made sure I got the best vehicle for the job, even when he had to send the chassis to another town for a custom body. He was all about making sure my needs were met. The fellow I bought cars from was like that too. Although these men worked at separate dealerships, they must have gone to the same school to learn to sell.

I remember the time I took delivery of my new 1982 luxury automobile. After I had signed all the paperwork and paid for the car, the salesman took 15 or 20 minutes to show me every feature of the new car and to take me for another test drive. Every time I had my car serviced it also got washed. And he either gave me a new one to drive or took me back to my office.

Both dealerships were friendly places with no appearance of confrontational situations. As far as I knew, neither of these fellows had a manager of any sort. There was no 'back and forth' and very little negotiating. They always had the figures within my expectations when they came to my office with their proposals.

I'm glad my car salesperson is like that today. Every time I have the itch for a new automobile, I call him. We email and talk on the phone several times about equipment and pricing before I ever go to his store since he's 90 miles from me. He and I have been doing this for a while so he knows what I like and how much I like to spend. We never waste time playing diversionary games. We handled the transaction on the last car I bought from him in less than half an hour. Washing and prepping the car actually took longer than making the deal.

Customers prefer a salesperson that makes the buying process easy. Though I consider myself a strong negotiator and master salesman, I don't like being the customer when the salesman is giving me a big helping of brain damage. When customers become burdened with a complicated or uncomfortable sales process, they start looking for ways to get out of it. They forget about buying and focus on escape. They use phrases like "Do you have a card? I need to think it over. I'll be back." They will throw your card away, never give you another thought and will certainly not be back.

How easy is your buying process? The easier it is to buy from you, the more cars you will sell and the more gross profit you will hold on each transaction. The easier it is to handle service of a vehicle purchased from you, the more often your client will bring their car back to your dealership for service rather than taking it to the local 'grease-n-go'. The more often your client does service business at your dealership, the more likely their next purchase will be made with you.

So are you making it easy to do business with you? If you're in the car business, do you focus on ways to help the client relax so you can determine their expectations? Do you listen carefully to their likes and dislikes, their proposed use and budget for the new vehicle? Or do you simply focus on gaining control of the sales process and press toward getting a commitment? The customer can tell if you're trying to manipulate them. People already have a prejudice when it comes to car people, so they're on the lookout for red flags as they 'swim with the sharks'.

A Customer Is A Person

Customers don't understand what a 'sales tower' is or why you may walk out of your office and your manager may walk in and take over their buying process. This is complicated! "What happened to the salesman", they wonder, "Let's get out of here! Ask him for his card! Tell him we need to go home and think about it!" When your customer spends an hour with you looking at cars, they begin to know you. But they don't know your manager. Every time you leave them to go to the tower, you lose gross profit.

Donald and I worked together at one of the greatest cars stores in America. It wasn't great because of inventory or pricing, it was great because of guys like Donald. He loved his customers and was very protective of them. Donald hovered over his customers like a mother hen. If his customer was required to meet another company person during the sales process, we all knew you were to wait until Donald introduced them. During the customer's ownership cycle, Donald was always their contact at the dealership. And every customer of Donald's could buy! Granted, some of them had credit issues that rendered them ineligible for our financing options. But Donald established a relationship with a 'buy-here-pay-here' dealer specifically for that client. Donald never told people 'no'. His customers never had a problem Donald could not handle. No wonder his customers will only buy from him!

Don't Steal The Trade-In

Customers don't understand why you offer them so little for their trade-in, yet you want so much for your new or used car. Do you make it a practice of explaining things and educating them, or do you press with all your Seminar closes until they give in or until they become so angry they'd like to punch you in the nose?

Wise automotive sales professionals realize the customer did not come to your dealership today because he is in love with his trade-in. Most likely, he didn't decide to go to your dealership and sell his trade-in to you today either. He may have gone online and looked up the value of his trade. Of course, that value is usually off since it is established monthly and changes in vehicle value occur daily in the car business. Further, the online figure is established regionally, and the same used car may bring hundreds more or less in a different section of that particular region. So when the customer flies off after you tell him what you'll pay for his trade, realize this has nothing to do with you. You simply need to take a little time and kindly explain how the appraiser arrived at that figure. Realize also that your customer wants a new vehicle, not the same one they drove onto the lot. The most frustrated customer in the world is the one who spends a couple of hours with a car salesman, and then drives back home in the same old car he left with.

Happy Birthday To Your Car

Hal sells luxury vehicles and trucks in Elizabeth City North Carolina. He's very successful and according to a survey taken by a local newspaper, the most respected car salesman in his market. When I met Hal, he had been in the business for about 4 or 5 years. He was working hard to build a client base through follow-up. Over fifteen years later, Hal is the king of follow-up! His customer base is enviable and more active than just a list of names. Once a year, you get a birthday card for your car from Hal. Hardly a week goes by that you don't hear someone in Hal's market marveling at the fact his or her car got a birthday card! Every quarter, you get a newsletter from Hal. He knows your trade cycle and contacts you prior to the time when you usually start shopping for something new. He may even bring a new car to your office or home when it's time to start car shopping! You won't find Hal working 12 hours a day, 7 days a week either. He 's very involved with his family and is a very active deacon in the largest church in town. Hal is living proof that success in the car business is about accomplishment, and not about activity. It isn't the number of hours you work; it's how many clients you regularly serve and keep in contact with.

Help Everybody, Not Just This Buyer

Back when that salesman sold me that 1964 Dodge, I was on top of the world. It was black with red interior and made the most awesome sound! There is no sound like the sound a high performance V-8 makes when it goes through glass pack mufflers. Suppose the salesman had asked me on the day I took delivery for the name of a friend who might be in the market for a car? Suppose he had sent me a card or given me a call thanking me for buying from him and asked me for a referral? I would have gladly told him several names!

Shoppers who come to you as a referral from a buyer are 3 times more likely than other customers to purchase from you. This means your 20% closing ratio can become 60% through focusing on referrals. Do you ask your buyers for referrals? And if you do ask, do you contact the referral? And when the referral comes in to shop, do you provide them with the very best level of service?

These are three reasons most people in the car business have few referrals; they don't ask for them, they don't promptly contact, they don't make the referred customer feel exceptional. Remember, people want to buy from an insider. You're the insider! Help them out!

One noteworthy fact about the automotive professionals like Donald and Hal and the fine fellow I buy from, they have little or no time to run all over the lot chasing 'ups'. They are busy staying in contact with their many clients and contacting all the referrals they receive every day.

Chapter Eight

Your Price Is Too High

Hesitation During The Buying Process

Since the dawn of time, man has looked back to yesterday and longed for the way things were back then. Salespeople know this like no other group of folk!

No matter your product or service, someone you call on today will tell you "That's too much! I can buy it over in another place for less."

In the early 1990's, very few Americans would even consider owning a particular Korean brand automobile. If you were in the car business, you didn't want to trade for one because you knew that no matter what you invested in the trade you would lose money when you took it to the used car auction. Americans perceived that particular Korean brand automobile to be an inferior product because it was priced so far below other cars.

I can't be sure of why the executives at that particular Korean brand automobile manufacturer's headquarters decided to enter the market at the low end, but I'd be willing to bet a salesperson was in the mix somewhere. We in the sales profession hear the price objection several times every day and we often wish for a product priced so low that no customer will ever again say our product is priced too high! All of our advertising mentions price. We boldly claim we will beat any price! Some of us even guarantee we'll pay the customer if they can find a price lower than ours! We want the world to know we have the lowest price and the lowest interest rates necessary to finance the purchase of our product.

Something changed at that particular Korean brand automobile's marketing headquarters though. Around the turn of the century that particular Korean brand automobile's marketing department introduced several new products. Some were priced way down low like the ones we already knew so well, but the new product line included medium priced products as well as a more luxurious product. The new products were priced barely below the competition's already successful products. When I wrote this book in 2006, that particular Korean brand automobile was a fast moving product! One great reason Americans took time to consider that particular Korean brand automobile as they shopped was that particular Korean brand automobile was priced just below the competition. The American consumer reasoned, "you get what you pay for", so that particular Korean brand automobile must be OK! If you doubt it look around in the mall parking lots and notice the cars on the freeway. Many are that particular Korean brand automobile.

Price Is Never The Problem

Was the early particular Korean brand automobile an inferior product? Is the new product line superior? Or does it matter at all?

The answer is, "It doesn't matter!" With today's technology and regulatory structure, there are no bad cars. If consumers perceive your product as worthwhile, quality isn't an issue. Their perception of your product's worth is what brings them to your location in the marketplace. Someone has told them about your product or they have seen some convincing information about why it is of value to them so they have decided to examine your product for themselves. So they come to your store and talk with you or invite you to come and talk with them so they can hear the story and figure out what is involved in their acquiring one. If nobody ever examines your product or tests it or asks you for a quote, the very best product in the world is still a dead duck. People must be attracted to your product before they will gain enough information to purchase your product.

In other words, people want value more than they want low price. You can have the very best price in the world on Whale Oil but if nobody needs it, nobody comes to your store looking for it. To the consumer, product value simply means "My life will be better when I own this". We all want our lives to be better. Americans will always buy something they truly want. And they will truly want something they feel is valuable. Even though the product may be expensive, Americans will find a way to purchase it. We finance expensive and luxurious automobiles for five or six years when we could easily pay cash for an old model with high mileage. We finance our comfortable large homes for thirty years when we could easily pay cash for a shack. We take the leap into debt because we feel there is value that equals or exceeds the price of this product, or because our neighbor has one and we want to own a bigger one.

Remember, value is what the client gets. Value is NOT what the salesman gets or what the studies report. Value is personal! What do I care if the guy who sold me a new boat won a trip to Miami? I care that I got my boat and it has all the bells and whistles I demanded! What do I care if a manufacturer is buying business with a $5,000.00 rebate and a dealer is buying business with a $5,000.00 discount on the truck I'm using to pull the boat? I'm going to tell all my buddies the window sticker was $45,000.00. In my mind, the truck is a $45,000.00 truck!

Notice and remember, clients refer to value not price! Even when they argue that you had better give them the best price, they will only buy if the product reflects the most value.

Everything Costs Too Much

A sales trainer from South Carolina often tells the story of a Mercedes Salesperson closing a car deal with a customer who felt the price was too high. The customer loudly remarked, "Your price is too high!" The customer went on to make his case about how he could buy a Cadillac or a Lincoln for thousands less. "Why even the Lexus dealer has your deal beat by several thousands!" he panted. The Mercedes Salesperson quietly allowed the customer to finish their rant, then looked them in the eye and said, "That's the very reason you will buy the Mercedes – because of its high value. Cadillac, Lincoln and Lexus are certainly fine automobiles. I'm sure you know several people who drive them. But you're shopping with me today because you won't be satisfied with anything less than the very best. I would feel mighty guilty knowing you had to settle for less simply because I didn't insist on your driving the finest motorcar in the world. You've earned the right to be a Mercedes owner. You deserve a Mercedes. Now, let's finish this paperwork and get you your Mercedes." Yes. The customer left the dealership in his new Mercedes.

The only reason to lower the price of your product is to compete with a financial proposal given to your client by a competitor. The established price of a mass produced product is set by the market and based on what buyers are already paying for the product in the marketplace.

Lowering the price lowers the perceived value of the product. Imagine spending the evening dining in the most elegant restaurant in your town. You have carefully chosen the restaurant to be the location where you will become engaged to the love of your life. Every detail has been addressed. From the crisp linen napkins to the crystal champagne glasses to the fine china, every elegant appointment imaginable is on display. As the two of you dine, the violinists stroll near your table and play softly as you gaze at each other through the glow of the candles. Finally, just before dessert, the question and perfect answer pass across the table. What a night! You have made certain this is a night to be remembered for a lifetime.

Just before you leave, the waiter brings the check. Would you attempt to negotiate with the waiter? Of course not! That would cheapen the special tone of the evening. You might even leave a hundred-dollar tip!

Now think of your customer purchasing your product. If yours is a product whose purchase price traditionally is negotiated, remember the engagement dinner. Your customer will ultimately purchase your product at some price if you've done a good job of presenting its features and benefits.

When the customer hesitates, rather than focusing on the price, remember that value attracts. Certainly salespeople need to bargain with customers on traditionally negotiated items but they don't need to give the products away!

There are two reasons for your customer to pay a price for your product that includes a fair profit. First, the ultimate price represents the true value of the product. If the price is reduced drastically, the customer views the product as initially overpriced. They may even feel they have done you a favor by purchasing it! A customer making this sort of purchase will never view the product as valuable. They will find fault with everything possible about the product. After all, they bought it off the discount table! It was a leftover, marked down with the discontinued items. Their Customer Satisfaction Survey will reflect a disrespect for the product and perhaps even for the sales staff. And they bought it at COST! They should be elated! They got a deal! Help your client purchase a product of high value.

The second reason for your customer to pay a price for your product that includes a fair profit is that you deserve to earn a fair living for helping your customers get your product. Salespeople work diligently at finding the correct product or service to fit each customer's needs. And the needs of each customer are unique. Admit it, you've served a client recently who put you through the paces and rewarded you with a nice order! At the close of that successful transaction, the sense of satisfaction exceeded even the nice commission. Some may reason that selling is an easy way to make a living. They've never worked in sales. Work hard for your clients! Serve them well! And allow them the honor of retaining your services as their insider. After all they're going to brag to their friends that they do business with you. Since your customer has now found an insider in your industry, they deserve the satisfaction of knowing they had to make an investment in order to have the very best.

We are particular about who we hire as a landscaper or carpenter. Since our home is our castle, it's worth paying the little extra required to hire a professional in order to avoid having to hire someone else to do things over after we saved a few bucks with cheap labor. Remember that when the client tells you your price is higher than your competition. While there's nothing to gain by berating your competition, there's also nothing to be gained by joining their price ranks.

Remember the words of the Mercedes salesman; "You're shopping with me today because you won't be satisfied with anything less than the very best. I would feel mighty guilty knowing you had to settle for less."

If You Argue, You Lose

When a customer feels passionate enough to argue with you, they are ready to buy. If they really could care less about owning your product, they would never confront you concerning the price or the other things customers argue about with sales people. Customers who don't want to buy will not interact with the salesperson.

The customer who says, "I had one of those once and it didn't last" is really asking, "Will this one last?" The customer who says, "I heard some bad things about your product or your company" is really saying, "I want to buy from you. Please tell me the negative things are unfounded that people say about your product or your company. Give me some logic to share with my boss when I'm challenged on this decision."

In other words, the customer who argues is really asking for enough information to justify the purchase. They really want to purchase. But they need some information you have not yet shared with them.

If you argue with a customer who is arguing with you, you will only further frustrate the customer. This sort of response to a person who is criticizing your product or you personally goes against human nature! It's natural to want to argue with an argumentative person, especially when they are telling you something you don't want to hear. Professional sales people must discipline themselves if they are to provide outstanding customer service.

Remember, our job is to help the customer get the product. We must get past the personal discomfort of hearing negative information, and we must listen to what the customer is really saying.

We must employ the 'who, what, when, where, why or how' questions and let the customer sound off. The only control we should exercise over the customer is to ask the right questions so they will open up and tell us what it will take to earn their business.

Once we know that, we must do a better job of informing the client of how this product will do what they want done, or we must inform them of the reasons they don't need to be concerned about the matter that is holding them back from the purchase.

Gather Information

If you sell using the techniques this book recommends, your presentations will be different than those of some of your peers who follow the same outline with each client. Sometimes, your client will only require a small amount of your product knowledge in order to decide to purchase. Sometimes, they will need more. Personalizing each sales presentation means we don't tell each client the same thing, but we address the client's needs, wants and expectations individually.

Sometimes a concern arises in the course of the presentation or sometimes the client is holding information back from us. Some clients will let us spend an hour with them before they will ever tell us what they truly want.

Successful sales professionals must tell themselves often that it is their responsibility to cause information to flow in the sales process. Clients are not responsible for sharing information with salespeople. Salespeople are responsible for comfortably extracting that information from the client. Clients are not responsible to be open and honest with salespeople. Salespeople are responsible for employing non-invasive ways to get at the vital truth.

If you ask a customer how their credit is, which is an illegal question by the way, they will most likely give you an incorrect answer. Lots of people really don't know how they look on the screens of the major reporting agencies. And those who know they look less than favorable will never tell you how bad they really are.

On the other hand, if a client tells you they have their current product financed with First National Bank and you casually ask, "How do you like dealing with them", you'll hear what sort of payment habits they have. What does it mean if the client says, "they worry me to death"? Is this a possible clue about their credit score? Why would a bank worry someone to death?

Objections usually occur at the moment of truth. By now, usually a presentation has been made and the client has been giving you encouraging feedback. You've spent enough time together to realize the client is truly interested in your product. Yet when you ask them to buy they say, "I need to think it over." Or they may say, "Your product will never work in my situation."

Bare in mind, this is at the end of a full presentation! Why did the client enter into this conversation if the product was not practical? The product IS practical and the client DOES want it. Something overwhelming in their mind needs to be satisfied before they can go ahead with the commitment. What is it?

Ask Until You Know

When a client says, "I need to think it over", wise sales professionals often respond in a kind voice with, "What is there to think over" or "You seem to be concerned about this purchase. What particular thing concerns you?" In other words, they ask why everything that was moving so well is at a halt!

Be careful how you handle client hesitation and objections.

In the early 1970's one of the major American truck manufacturers introduced a mini pickup to their truck line and I decided I had to own one. I shopped around until I found one I liked, and then offered my foreign work car as a trade-in. I don't know why the salesman didn't want me to test-drive the little truck before he asked me to buy it but that was what happened.

I was wondering how the truck would drive. Also, I'd heard the little trucks didn't have sufficient power to be safe on the freeway. When I told the salesman I didn't think the little truck would have the power to handle my needs, he quoted the horsepower specifications and told me it had more power than my little foreign work car. I said, "I can't buy a truck I've never driven!" So he asked me, "Is that all you need to do in order to buy this truck?" What do you say to that sort of question? Like a typical shopper, I said, "Sure! Now let me test drive the truck!" So he did.

When I returned from test-driving, which I did by myself, the salesman called me into his office and asked me to sign a buyers order. No mention had been made of figures, so I said I still wasn't ready to trade. At this, he left the office and his manager stormed in. And I mean he stormed in!

Not only was the manager wearing clothes he should have replaced 20 pounds ago, he was wearing wrap-around dark glasses. He leaned across the table toward me and barked, "You lied to the salesman! You said you would buy the truck if you drove it! Now, after you drove it, you won't buy it! You're a liar!" I was a macho young Air Commando Vietnam Veteran, so my first impulse was to introduce him to my 'whip the tar out of you' instant weight loss program. He followed up with, "You were going to buy, now you're not going to buy. Something changed! What changed? I want to know right now!"

In my mind, this transaction was history. I quickly got the keys to my little foreign work car and headed out the door.

How could the salesman have saved this transaction when I hesitated, after we had been standing there talking positively about the truck for over half an hour? When I told him I needed to drive the truck in order to buy it, he should have asked me, "Why is driving the truck important to you?" He should have asked me enough questions to determine exactly what was causing me to hesitate. He also should have accompanied me on the test-drive and asked me for feedback as I drove, "What do you think about the power? Does this seem to be strong enough to handle the traffic you drive your work car in right now? Is this what you're looking for?"

Please remember that we are not to argue with argumentative clients. When the manager came in to handle what the salesman couldn't, he should have started by finding out why I would not commit. Was it because I didn't like the truck? Was it because the figures were not to my liking? Was it something the salesman said or did?

An objection is a buying signal. The client has granted you an interview, been with you all the way though the sales process, given you feedback during your presentation and now says they have a concern. This is great news! All you need to do in order to secure his business is handle the concern!

Remember that most clients are not professional communicators. They don't know how to express to you that they really want the product without leaving themselves open to one of your powerful closes. So they beat around the bush or appear to be confrontational.

The first order of business is to understand why the client is holding back. Ask. Most often, that starts the ball rolling. The client is dying to buy the product but they don't want to make a mistake and they obviously feel they would be making a mistake by buying at this point. So what's the concern?

Using the 'who, what, when, where, why or how' questions, get the client to tell you exactly what they are concerned about. Keep on asking and letting the client explain until you are convinced you can calm their fears.

But don't answer the concern or objection yet! You need one more vital bit of information.

Why Do You Think That?

Most client concerns are based on misunderstand or lack of information concerning your product. If they knew what you know about the product, they'd buy it.

Perhaps some acquaintance bought one and it didn't work right. Or daddy knows a guy who sells them and the client really feels obligated to give that person a chance at their business. In the case of a corporate account, the boss has given your client some requirement different from the solution you and the client have agreed upon, and now they must be prepared to defend this change in direction. The key here is that a friend, family member or person of importance has influenced the client's decision.

Once again, in order to gather information, we must get the client to talk with us.

Wise sales professionals often ask, "Where did you get this information" or "What makes you think this" or "Who told you that". Once again, the purpose of this question is to gather information for the purpose of helping the client get the product. It is not for the purpose of finding someone to blame.

If you show the client all the convincing information in the world and if you make the most compelling case for buying, yet you unknowingly challenge or insult his source for having this concern, you have lost the sale.

In order to successfully handle a customer concern that is generated by information from a third party, you must lend credibility to the third party while building a strong case for going ahead with the purchase. Your customer already thinks enough of the third party's opinion to stop the buying process based upon their opinion. At this point, the third party trumps you.

If a customer tells you the neighbors said your roofing crew dropped debris all over the yard when you replaced their roof and they don't want the same to happen to them, calling the neighbor a liar will kill the deal. Even if the neighbor is wrong, you must begin by finding a way to complement the neighbor. "You have a good neighbor to be so concerned for your welfare" sounds lots better than, "That's not true!" Even if you never directly address what the third party has said, you should find some nice thing to say about them. Later, when the client defends their buying decision to the third party, one of the first things they'll tell them is, "The salesman said nice things about you!" This is especially true when the third party is another salesman from a competing company.

Asking the 'who, what, when, where, why or how' questions, get the client to explain their feelings about the source of the information. Keep on asking and letting the client explain until you are convinced your words will not create a confrontation between you and the third party, or between the client and the third party.

This Is The Only Thing Holding Us Back, Right?

One of the most uncomfortable customer phrases at this delicate point in the sales process is, "and another thing!" This leaves the sale unclosed no matter how many times you put your client's mind at ease about their concerns.

Once you feel totally confident in handling the concern and it's source, look the client in the eye and say, "So the only thing holding you back from hiring me to re-roof your home today is that you want to make sure your lawn and driveway stay clean and free of debris, is that right?"

Look the client in the eye and respectfully wait for the answer for as long as it takes.

Notice the question is asked in a positive way. Avoid asking negative questions unless you are tired and want to hurry up and lose this sale so you can go home.

The customer is thinking about what you are saying. You have no idea, which words will be the ones he hangs on. Make your words positive.

The customer's answer should also be positive. If your client says, "That's right" or "I'd say that pretty much sums it up", they're focused on making a purchase and simply need assurance that this is the right one to make. If the answer is, "No" or "It isn't that simple" or even "You wish", go back to clarifying exactly what the client is concerned about. Remember the 'who, what, when, where, why or how' questions. This time, listen intently for whatever you missed the first time.

I Need More Time

Sometimes you may encounter a client that truly needs time in order to make a decision. High-ticket items and personal commitments frequently enter this category. How the client leaves you to go and do their thinking is extremely important. Make sure they have sufficient information to make an informed decision. Also, make sure a firm follow-up date is agreed upon before they leave.

Extending courtesy to a client who must think it over is unusual so they will remember you. Most salespeople aren't going to be inclined to let a client leave without some sort of commitment. Some will actually sit there with the client and try their best to coerce the client or even buy their business by repeatedly lowering the price. This is especially true in major markets where high volumes of anonymous clients shop establishments. Some industries repeatedly turn clients over to other salespeople or managers in order to wear the client down.

While worn-out clients will eventually buy, they often experience buyers' remorse and they seldom result in becoming high-profit or repeat clients. Besides, in the time it takes to wear one client out, successful sales professionals can meet with several other clients and make multiple sales.

In my automotive sales career, letting a client take the proposed figures and drive the new car home overnight to think about it sold many cars. Even when a client came in the next morning and said they could beat my price at another dealership, the sale was made since the client had established more trust with our company than with the stranger on the phone.

Once I overheard a couple telling a salesman they needed to pray before they could decide about buying a new car. The salesman got up, walked around his desk, took each of their hands and said, "Fine! Let's pray right now!" If a client says they need to go home and pray about a purchase, they are never going to decide before they have time to pray. People who pray about major decisions actually see the salesman's urge to rush the process as a clear sign that they should not buy from him.

If you establish a strong professional relationship with your client, you'll know whether they need time to decide. If they need time, give it to them. You're going to be selling products for a long time. You're in no rush.

Put Them Out Of Their Misery

When I was relatively new to the car business, my friend Bruce once told me to go put a difficult client out of his misery. Having grown up around a farm, you know what came to my mind. "Shame on you, Bruce! I'm not going to go in there and shoot the client!"

The fact is people who want your product and get to the moment of truth only to hesitate or object are miserable! They want to buy it and go home! Instead they're still talking with the salesman. Usually about money! And the reason not to buy is almost never money.

Just as it is your responsibility to gather the necessary information to facilitate a sale, it is your responsibility to persist until the client can rest in ownership. Lots of people tell retail salespeople they are 'just looking' when they are really looking for someone to sell them what they want so they can go home and enjoy it.

The greatest kindness you can show to a client who has spent time with you and listened to your presentation only to hesitate or decline your offer, is to put their mind at ease about their concerns and help them get the product.

Some salespeople actually say they didn't close a deal because they didn't want to put pressure on the client. I'll tell you what pressure is. Wanting a new boat and spending an hour with a boat salesman, only to go home with no new boat! Of course, I did tell the salesman I wasn't sure I could afford the boat because it was priced a little higher than I thought it would be. That was when the boat salesman said, "I know what you mean. Well, think it over and get back to me if you decide you can afford it." So Saturday morning all my neighbors hook their boats to their trucks and head for the water. But not me! I don't have a boat! Now that's pressure!

What if the salesman had said to me, "You don't have to pay for it all at one time! Let's let the bank decide what you can afford. You'll be surprised how easy it is to have just the boat you want and deserve!"

Your customer wants your product. Help them get it!

If a customer hesitates or declines your offer, they will need new and different information in order to make a positive decision. If you tell them the same thing again and again, they will feel the same way and give you the same decision over and over. This is a great reason to make customized presentations to customers. You never give all your information away. The salesperson who spouts all the information they know about a given product to every customer they talk to is in trouble when an objections arises because they have nothing new to share with the client.

As you handle their concern, sell them on the features or benefits that outweigh their concerns. As you share information with the client, ask for feedback as you did during the sales process. Feedback is especially crucial now. Watch the client's body language. Listen to the client's words.

When you sense the client is comfortable owning the product, ask them to buy. Any time you handle a concern or overcome an objection, you must ask for commitment. Failure to do so will cause the client to go to your competitor as soon as possible and buy. After all, you've removed the roadblock to the purchase.

Someone else will always have a lower price and a product that will do something your product cannot do. Someone else will always have a better idea or better journalistic influence resulting in flattering write-ups in magazines.

Your customer is talking to you because they firmly believe your product to be the ideal product for their personal situation, regardless of the other choices.

Don't make him settle for second best, simply because you didn't persist.

CHAPTER NINE

Moving Into Management

Bill and 'Old Sarge'

One of the great salesmen I met in my life was an Air Force General named William P Acker. General Acker was a dynamic fellow with a hero's history as a fighter pilot and commander of Air Force fliers. A hero of the Vietnam war, he was also noted as Commander of Air Force Recruiting and later Commander of Air Force Military Training Center where enlisted folks go through Air Force Basic Training. He went on to command Air Force Air Training Command, which was over both of those organizations, as well as the initial training and individual skills training for enlisted and officers in the Air Force.

I loved talking with him since he was such a down-to-earth fellow for someone who was so accomplished. Not only was he a great friend to many people, he was one of the most gifted speakers I've heard. Whether he was speaking to a group of Air Force Recruiters or Drill Sergeants, he seemed to always work in his story about 'Old Sarge'. I can never do it justice the way Bill Acker can, but let me relate the main idea of this amusing tale.

Some wealthy business owners had a traditional annual trip to enjoy bird hunting in Texas. Their guide had a very spirited dog named, 'Old Sarge'. 'Old Sarge' was faster and more focused than any hunting dog the businessmen had ever seen. 'Old Sarge' would hop out of the truck and go straight to the location of the birds on point. On command, he would consistently scare the birds into flight and immediately fetch any kills (never missing or damaging a single bird). One of the business owners, a self made millionaire and world-class hunter, remarked that 'Old Sarge' was the most outstanding dog he had ever hunted with!

Year after year, the growing number of businessmen would come back to hunt with the guide and 'Old Sarge'. Year after year, 'Old Sarge' performed beyond belief. One year, an Air Force General in the hunting party and was duly impressed with the outstanding feats of this Non-Commissioned Dog. The General, a veteran of World War II, related that outstanding Non-Commissioned Officers such as Audie Murphy, were rewarded for their performance above and beyond the call of duty on the battlefield with an on-the-spot commissioning to officer rank. The businessmen and the General suggested such an action was in order for 'Old Sarge'! The guide, a civilian not quite grasping what all this meant, agreed never the less. With pomp and formality, the General gave 'Old Sarge' a battlefield commission and made him a Lieutenant! A new brass tag was ordered and 'Lieutenant' assumed his new identity.

The following year the businessmen and the General returned for yet another great hunting outing with the dog of all dogs. As the guide loaded the truck with 3 new dogs, they asked, "Where's 'Lieutenant'? You know, 'Old Sarge', the dog with the battlefield commission?"

The guide replied, "That dog won't hunt anymore. Ever since he became an officer, he just sits on his rear-end and barks."

General Acker was famous for the way he could tell this story, and for the way it would cause an audience of enlisted men and women to roar with laughter. He was also famous for the way the officers in his command were committed to the mission and involved as effective managers and leaders.

If you're a professional who has never worked in sales management, you may feel this story is representative of sales managers. After all, they call all the shots. They hold our feet to the fire and make us do as we're told. And they have those heart-to-heart talks with us when our numbers are low. It almost seems they don't work at all except to sit on their rear-ends and bark at us for something.

It is possible for great sales people to fail as managers. It is also possible for weak salespeople to succeed in sales management. The key word here is "possible". More likely, an individual with a successful sales background leads a winning sales team. Sales management is actually just another type of selling – the manager sells the staff on following his lead. Sales professionals require a successful sales-oriented leadership style. And great sales managers handle company leadership (their superiors) with the same concern and gracefulness that they employed with their clients back when they were successfully selling in the field.

Outstanding sales professionals who understand the principals of leadership and who are committed to the success of the team are excellent leadership candidates.

But moving into sales leadership is something that should not be taken lightly. Just as most people are not cut out for a career in sales, many sales professionals are not cut out for a sales management position. I invite you to think about some things before you move into the big office at corporate headquarters.

The Financial Impact

Typically, the highest paid individual on a sales team is NOT the manager. Occasionally the manager is paid more than any person on the team, but more often one or two outstanding producers among the sales professionals will exceed the manager's income level due to their commitment to closing high-dollar accounts (and lots of them).

The Financial Decision should be considered prior to a move from sales to sales management. Wise companies pay their sales managers a salary plus override (percentage of the profits produced by their sales team). While the salary of a sales manager is often envious, the total manager's compensation package is seldom higher than the income of the top producer on the team. Some outstanding financially motivated sales professionals refuse the offer to move up, simply because they prefer the luxury of consistent high income.

From time to time, certain factors cause a poor performance of the sales staff. Whether these factors are the result of a poor effort on the part of the sales staff or some sudden economic impact on your market and client base, the result is right there in your check. Meanwhile, you're the coach who must fix the financial situation.

As a sales professional calling on clients, you can make as many calls as is necessary and work as many hours as it takes to get your numbers up right away. As the manager, you are tasked with successfully motivating and enabling others in order to achieve this goal. Sales managers who themselves resort to selling in order to reach team goals are only shorting themselves and poorly serving their company and would-be clients. Effective sales managers keep their numbers up by correctly directing the efforts of the correct number of properly motivated sales professionals. The duty of the coach is to call the plays, not to run them.

Are you aware you may not be the highest paid individual aboard? How do you feel about that? Is your income level a matter of ego or is it a matter of 'making a comfortable living'? How do you feel about someone else serving your clients from now on? Do you have faith in the sales team to achieve the objectives necessary in order to achieve the override that will maintain your comfortable standard of living? Should your income fall, do you possess the necessary skill and patience to help your team get the numbers back up? Does your spouse realize the financial implications, positive and negative, of this move?

The Geographical Impact

Some prefer the regimen of working directly with clients rather than being limited to interaction between company leadership and sales professionals.

An Air Force Recruiter was able to play golf a couple of days each week when the course was relatively empty since he was exceeding his goals and had the free time during the day. But when he moved into management, he no longer had the free time to do such things.

Face the fact that in management you will be spending much more time in the office and your office will likely be in a place where people are accustomed to normal hours and corporate disciplines. Also, your responsibilities will greatly increase so you will have far less free time than you do as a sales representative.

The Thinking Impact

You may be the type of person who actually needs this lifestyle. Management types are more fulfilled when they are directing the efforts and solving the problems of a sales force. While a management type may function as a pretty good salesperson, they excel as a sales manager because leadership is their passion.

On the other hand, just because a person is an outstanding sales representative is no indication that they will excel as a sales manager. While a background in selling is a must in order for a sales manager to succeed, an outstanding sales record is no guarantee that a person will excel as a sales manager.

Some enter management and continue to think like sale people. Not only do they sell their sales staff on daily goals and activities, which is good, but they also continue to work their old accounts. A decision must be made when you move into management. You must decide to cross the bridge and not go back. If the current sales force cannot properly handle your old accounts, you need to hire a new salesperson to take care of them. The accounts belong to the company and as the manager; you must assure all accounts are addressed in order to achieve maximum results.

As a manager, you're responsible for the success of your sales force. This means you must analyze the needs of the company, the needs of the sales force, plan and execute accordingly.

Do your 5 sales people need to sell 100 items? Then each of them must sell an average of 20. Some will sell fewer and some will sell more. You must plan and correct ahead of time for this inevitable fact.

Do the salespeople require special training in order to accomplish their sales goals or to use a new piece of equipment or technology? You must arrange for that training or conduct it yourself.

Do the salespeople need equipment or special funding in order to accomplish sales goals? You must sell corporate on granting this funding. That is often your hardest deal to close. Corporate is already upset because the salespeople make so much money and have so much fun. Their jealousy, along with their ignorance of the importance of a properly equipped and properly motivated sales force will often give you gray hair.

Rather than being the shining star you were when you were closing all those record-breaking sales, you'll now spend many days selling corporate on simply doing the right thing. There will be little or no thanks, since your visionary thinking will usually be way ahead of what is actually going on. Your commitment will keep corporate in their plush surroundings and everyone down to the lowest paid employee will have security because you are thinking ahead. But if you don't do your job and keep your sales force fully equipped and motivated, the whole company will suffer.

These situations are very real and should be considered prior to a move to management.

Sales Manager - Coach And Cheerleader

Great managers are very much needed. Companies need them in order to consistently generate cash flow. Salespeople need them in order to plan and direct their efforts toward new and different ways of serving customers. Sounds almost like a mission statement, doesn't it?

Realizing that people move toward their current dominant thought, effective sales managers find ways to capture the thinking of the sales force and focus that thinking on financial victory for the company. Cash flow is now your specialty. You cause the sales force to sell products, resulting in billing and funding for the company. You design and structure incentives and commission scales, resulting in funding for the sales force. You hold the moneybag!

The quota drove every sales job I've ever had. The minimum acceptable number of sales or sales dollars was spelled out in a monthly letter from the sales manager. This is one of your responsibilities. When you establish the quota, be sure to factor in the likelihood of certain members of the sales force to fall short of their personal quota. Also, remember those deals that don't make, due to financing or other factors beyond your control. Better to ask the people to do more as a team than to sit with your hat in your hand and explain to corporate why you missed the goal.

What made you produce so well as a sales professional? That's a great place to start! The same incentive that drove you may drive others. Was something missing, or only appearing occasionally that caused you to do your best? Factor it in!

Is your team staffed with sufficient sales professionals to consistently produce 110% of the necessary cash flow? One faulty move made by some managers is to flood the sales force with bodies. They reason that more people sell more products, resulting in more cash flow. While this may look good on paper, it's sometimes counterproductive. Sales professionals are sometimes even de-motivated by the supply of clients being spread so thin that high income seems out of reach. Sometimes, it's more effective to offer higher incentives to 5 extremely productive salespeople than to pay the FICA, 401k and withholding on a 6th one of unknown value. The key qualifier to the effectiveness of such a decision is the bottom line. What is the final sales figure at the end of each month? Sometimes that figure is actually higher with fewer highly motivated people.

Are You Staffed With Employees Or Salespeople?

As the new coach, one of your first studies is to determine who the players are. Are you leading a team of employees or a team of sales professionals? You need to know this in order to properly manage their efforts as you work toward achieving the financial goals your company needs in order to survive and thrive.

Nothing is wrong with wishing to be an employee. Employees keep our companies moving ahead by doing the work. But employees don't pay the bills because they do not ask customers to purchase and pay. Salespeople do that. If you have employees asking customers to purchase and pay, you're over-tasking the employee and shortchanging your company. Employees are not hungry and are not driven to go above and beyond standards, or to persist when dealing with a difficult client. Thought they are excellent people who do their best, they do the human thing when dealing with difficult situations and difficult people. They flee.

But salespeople want to win. They press for the win, working with the client no matter how difficult or uncomfortable the situation may be. Because the sales professional is driven to win and because that professional is on commission, therefore will be paid more if the customer buys than if they do not, sales professionals are the best candidates for sales positions.

Some will argue that they want the security of a salary so they will not have to worry about making enough income to pay their obligations. With the proper person in the properly structured commission package, they will routinely earn more commission than the manager can ever justify as a salary. Occasionally sales people need to be shown this fact on paper, especially when sales are low.

Train Salespeople To Self-Manage

Although many help-wanted ads contain the phrase, "must be able to multi-task", people can only do one thing at the time very well. Your sales force is no exception. If they are to succeed, they must spend a great deal of time successfully selling. Which means they cannot spend a lot of time being managed.

Several industries are overboard with micromanagement of sales people. Companies require salespeople to spend hours interacting with managers concerning what they're going to say to a client or what they said and what the client said back. When you factor in all the time necessary to write up the daily sales log, stating every action of every minute of the salesperson's day, very little time is left for actually doing what a salesperson is to do – sell!

Of all the actions you take, how many cause the salesperson to actually close sales? You're the cash flow expert. If the things you're doing don't cause cash to flow, maybe you'd be better off not doing them.

How many mandatory meetings result in more closed sales? You're already at headquarters. You should go to the meeting and inform the sales force later when they're all together or through an email. Their best meetings are meetings with clients.

Sales professionals are independent by nature so encourage and equip that independence. Make sure they are trained to the point of confidence in sales techniques, product knowledge and effective time management. Make sure they have all the equipment, communication and other, required to close the most sales in the least amount of time.

Avoid costing yourself and the company money by taking your cash producing sales force out of action for ego-stroking meetings. The more time you spend managing your sales professionals the less time they can spend closing sales and generating cash flow.

Incentives That Bring Sales Results

The subject of compensation requires your constant attention as a sales manager. While most managers of other departments handle the money question at the date of hiring, then once a year or so, sales managers handle it every day. The purpose of retaining the sales staff is to bring money to the company. The amount of money the sales staff is paid must be an asset to the company, not a liability. The sales staff's compensation must result in positive cash flow rather than show on the bottom line as a negative number.

If a mechanic's compensation package is $50,000.00 per year, the hiring will cost the company $50000 per year. If a sales professionals compensation package is $50,000.00 per year, that hiring must cause the company cash flow to increase noticeably more than $50,000.00 per year. Employees are expected to be an expense. Sales staff is expected to be an asset. The actual percentage of inflow caused by a successful sales person differs from industry to industry. But a salesperson that simply covers their salary is not pulling their share of the load.

The other part of the financial consideration when staffing a sales force is the package as seen through the eyes of the sales professional. Remember, selling is selling and successful sales professionals can sell anything. They are driven by the need to win and they love to win big contracts and cash in on big sales contests. The compensation package must be enough to retain them with the company, while competitors try to hire them away from you. Once you staff your sales force with the best sales professionals, everyone from your closest competitor to the company clients will be constantly be trying their best to hire your staff away from you.

Though sales professionals are not financially motivated, they are unlikely to leave the highest paying job in the market. If their commission is a higher percentage than any competitor offers and if their benefits outweigh the competition's packages by a noticeable margin, they are highly unlikely to leave.

Simple math will help you consistently offer competitive incentives to your sales force. Since you can only spend a dollar once, and since you are responsible for all inflow of dollars to your company, your incentives and commissions must be taken from funds above and beyond required company expenses. If the company requires $50,000.00 per month to operate, funds beyond $50,000.00 must be raised to pay commissions and incentives. The team sales goal must be higher than the minimum funds necessary to survive. Otherwise you will find yourself treading water until the creditors or the new sales manager get there, depending on the savvy of your company superiors.

In other words, with a sales force of 3 and a company need of $50,000.00, each salesman should be tasked with producing $20,000.00. One may do a little better than the others while one brings in a little less than his goal. A small percentage of the clients will be late on their payment, and some may cancel. That still leaves your company in the black numbers once those handsome commission checks, including yours, have been issued.

Compensation Structure

Salespeople perform best when compensated totally by commission. The more seasoned sales professionals become, the more they realize their income is driven by their activity and accepting a salary of any figure is tantamount to giving up income.

Further, sales professionals respond well to a graduated or sliding commission scale. In effect, the salesman is compensated a certain percentage of the profit (or some other figure such as total sales price, as in real estate). If each member your sales force is expected to sell $20,000.00 of business each month and the typical commission in your industry is 15%, a sliding scale could start at 15% commission on sales up to and including $20,000.00. If a salesman sees that sales above $20,000.00 will be compensated at 25% and sales above $30,000.00 will be compensated at 35%, the motivation is there and the results will naturally follow! Sales professionals who have been in the business for a long time prefer to work on full commission with no salary to confuse things.

Some prefer the comfort of a salary and the luxury of a commission. I like to call this 'having your cake and eating it too'. Should you decide to make such an arrangement with your sales force, the salary should not be a living wage. Remember, if the salesperson is hungry they will work to eat. If the base salary pays their bills, they aren't going to be motivated to do much more than the minimum. This arrangement is not the recommended approach if you wish your sales force to perform at peak.

It goes without saying that commission is paid on collected funds. Very few professional organizations pay commission on promises, which is what a signed contract amounts to. If your sales force is being paid on signed contracts with no money, your credit and collections staff is working overtime and your write-offs are likely above the desired level.

Sales professionals, who learn that their money flows only when the company receives money, will establish a habit of bringing money in with contracts. If you're facing a collections problem, examine your company policy regarding commissions. Are you rewarding people before they bring money to the table? Stop it now if you are!

Remember, company cash follow is the responsibility of the sales manager, not the credit manager.

Paying Incentives To NON-Sales Employees

Your sales force will certainly put their best foot forward at all times. They are respectful, professional, courteous and attentive to client needs. The occasion when a sales person insults a client is pretty rare. But sometimes other people from your company deal with the clients, if only for a minute or two.

When the client calls your company, who answers the phone? When your forklift driver loads the client's truck, does he talk with the client's driver? When the client is 45 days late paying their bill, who calls them? When your client requires service on their equipment, which of your staff interacts with the client? If your employees wear company uniforms, how do they conduct themselves in community establishments?

Since you are the guru of cash flow for your company, you may occasionally find the need to stoke the fires of other employees. While every person in your company who has contact with a client is actually representing the company and is indirectly involved in selling, most of them do not think like sales professionals. We've already established that a career in sales is not for everyone.

Sometimes we need the little added enthusiasm or extra customer-centered concern of all the employees to help the sales force put the numbers over the top. Money really talks in these situations, especially to non-commissioned people within a company.

The purpose of the incentive is to cause greater cash flow. Therefore, the incentive must be factored into the financial goal. As with the example of the salespeople, decide the total cost of the incentive and add that to the goal. If I am to pay each of my 50 employees $100 bonuses when we reach our $80,000.00 goal, I must add $5,000.00 to the $80,000.00 goal. So when I make the banners and send out the fliers and emails, the goal is $85,000.00! Reaching this goal will fulfill the financial need and pay for the incentive.

Incentives need to be flamboyant. If you are going to ask an employee to do something they wouldn't normally do, such as being extra attentive to client satisfaction or extremely polite when answering the phone, the reward needs to be something they wouldn't normally receive. I always liked giving away hundred dollar bills. There's something about getting a picture of Benjamin that just makes your day! And the sales manager or the company CEO should be the one to go from workstation to workstation and put the bill in the employee's hand, shake their hand and say "Congratulations on a job well done!"

By the way, employees must understand an incentive is not salary but a reward. It is not negotiable. If the goal is $85,000.00, reaching $84,900.00 nets the employee nothing. The goal is $85,000.00! Employees will not only learn the importance of getting the whole job done, they will have a renewed respect for the sales force.

The switchboard operator or shipping clerk may have never had a bonus check. The thought that reaching a certain financial goal will result in a bonus is intoxicating! Employees will find themselves being extra courteous and attentive to clients. You'll see the employees looking at the daily sales report in the break room. They may even ask the sales force if there is anything they need!

Warning! They can get hooked on this! Of course, that only means you have found something that works!

Power To The People

Many managers are not comfortable delegating, or equipping staff. They hold the reins of decision tightly and micromanage the activities of their sales force. Strangely enough, the same manager often seems to have no problem at all with holding the staff accountable. That approach is very confusing, since the team is being constantly held accountable for things over which they have little or no control.

If negotiation with clients is routine in your industry, sales professionals need to have the power to handle the negotiation without going back and forth or making several phone calls. If you send a person to do a job, equip them with the tools and with the authority they need in order to succeed. The more power your sales force has, the more they will accomplish.

And the more you can hold them accountable. If you give a person everything they need in order to succeed and they fail, you have a starting place to correct the problem or dismiss the person from your team.

Equipped people usually succeed! Micromanaged people usually fail!

Train your team. Equip your team. Authorize your team. Compensate your team.

The cash will then flow making you a management success.

About The Author

Tim Dannelly travels the United States as a Professional Speaker. He is the author of *Living the American Dream*, a book designed to inspire and empower people in leadership roles and those wishing to improve the quality of their lives.

He has well over thirty years experience in the areas of sales, public relations and broadcasting. His leadership and management exposure includes sales professionals, entertainers and specialized technicians.

Tim served in Virginia as a successful Air Force Recruiter, and was selected as a sales and public relations instructor by the elite Air Force Recruiting School. His duties introduced him as a speaker and sales trainer for annual meetings of Air Force Recruiters across the country.

Following his Air Force career, Tim pursued a sales career that involved intangibles, such as broadcast advertising, as well as the very tangible areas of real estate and new cars. In each sales endeavor, he quickly rose to management. He worked in the rapidly growing San Antonio real estate market and was a regular sales trainer for many Real Estate companies in Texas. He successfully managed several AM and FM radio stations, specializing in the "turnaround" of failing radio stations. Both General Motors and Chrysler Corporation cited his new vehicle sales teams for high sales achievements.

For more information contact;

Tim Dannelly

PO Box 1092

Edenton, NC 27932

Or visit

www.timdannelly.com

www.ingramcontent.com/pod-product-compliance
Lightning Source LLC
Chambersburg PA
CBHW030007190526
45157CB00014B/1006